Portfolio Assessment

Amy E. Seely, M.Ed.

Teacher Created Materials, Inc.

Illustrations by: Adam Doti

Made in U.S.A.
ISBN 1-55734-845-6

Order Number TCM 845

Table of Contents

Introduction i

Assessment Profile: What is Involved? 1

Moving From a Collection to Authentic Assessment 9

Guidelines for Portfolio Assessment Practices 23

Types of Portfolios: From Showcase to Process 35

Issues to Consider 45

Constructing Professional Development Portfolios 51

Portfolios Across the Curriculum 57

Last Thoughts, Future Directions 69

References 74

Introduction

Professional's Guide: Portfolio Assessment discusses and highlights portfolios as an alternative assessment practice in the classroom. The chapters address such topics as aspects of portfolios beyond a collection of student work, what to consider when evaluating portfolios, the different types and purposes of student portfolios, issues involving management and ownership of the portfolios, professional development portfolios, and integrating portfolio assessment throughout the curriculum. Throughout the chapters are examples of ways to integrate portfolio assessment practices into your own classroom. Sample forms are included to provide you with possibilities that may be useful for you and your students.

The underlying focus of *Professional's Guide: Portfolio Assessment* is to encourage discussion about ways in which portfolios are successfully implemented as alternative assessment practices in classrooms. As you read and reflect on the various chapters of the book, keep in mind portfolios offer glimpses into the thinking and learning of students and teachers. Portfolio assessment practices are multifaceted with many possibilities and pathways.

Assessment Profile: What is Involved?

What are Assessment Practices?

Assessment practices are embedded within our country's educational system. On any given instructional day, teachers and students engage in some aspect of assessment. Involved in assessment practices are activities in which a decision or judgment is being made regarding the performance of a student. Assessment practices are used in an effort to find the best fit for students and their educational environment (Smith, 1994). The fit should reflect students who are actively participating and challenged in their instructional programs. As a teacher, you will evaluate and judge your students on a variety of tasks and concepts throughout the instructional year. The decisions you make have far reaching implications for your students as they progress through their academic programs. Decisions made affecting level of instruction and/or placement into special programs are usually the most common outcomes of assessment practices. Teachers and others in the educational community frequently rely upon the results of assessment practices to determine the academic course for many students. Assessment practices, therefore, are important aspects of the educational system and play a critical role in the academic lives of your students and in your professional life as a teacher.

Decisions made affecting level of instruction and/or placement into special programs are the most common outcomes of assessment practices.

With the concept of assessment ingrained into our thinking about learning and teaching, the practices implemented in classrooms to evaluate student performance belong to one of two categories: formal and alternative. Formal, or standardized, assessment practices are used to determine and evaluate students' knowledge on specific skills and concepts. These formal assessment practices have served as the primary method of assessment for most of the twentieth century (Worthen, 1993). Formal assessment practices are in most cases identified as multiple-choice or true-false achievement tests. Achievement tests are the most widely used tests in schools, designed to assess what a student knows and can do as a result of schooling (U.S. Congress, Office of Technology Assessment, 1992). Students are expected to select a single correct answer in a specified amount of time. "Traditional tests often assess what is easy to test—memorization of rote skills and procedures" (California Mathematics Council, 1991, p. 2). The focus is on the product a student is capable of producing.

Alternative assessment practices include such methods as portfolios, performance-based activities, running re-cords, checklists, anecdotal records, observations, etc.

Standardized assessment practices use uniform procedures for administering and scoring. Individual student performance is often compared to the performances of a large group of students. The standards and criteria by which students are evaluated are established by outside agencies, such as test developers and publishers, measurement experts, and analysts. The standardized testing practices many of you are familiar with are not designed to make decisions regarding the progress of each individual student yet this is what generally happens. Standardized assessment practices are to be utilized in decisions involving curriculum and instructional programs for schools and/or districts, and to allocate educational resources and opportunities among students.

Alternative assessment practices, on the other hand, are interested in the learning processes students engage in, including the ways in which knowledge is represented, reorganized, and used to process new information. Alternative assessment practices involve many sources of information to evaluate student performance. Information is gathered from a variety of situations to better understand students' processes in thinking and learning. Alternative assessment practices include such methods as portfolios, performance-based activities, running records, checklists, anecdotal records, observations, etc. With alternative assessment practices, evaluation is perceived as part of the ongoing daily experience in the classroom (Goodman, 1991).

Alternative assessment practices utilize a variety of methods and procedures to gather and analyze information. With the variety of approaches to alternative practices, it is important to consider whether the practice is sound in the construction and implementation. Developing sound alternative assessment practices for the classroom require addressing four guiding principles. When making judgments regarding students' performances on various tasks and concepts Valencia (1990) has identified the four principles as: (1) anchored in authenticity, (2) continuous and ongoing, (3) multidimensional, and (4) providing active and collaborative reflection.

Alternative assessment practices are designed to evaluate student performance on an individual basis. These practices monitor and provide feedback on the educational progress of each student. Teachers interpret the gathered information according to their individual expectations of a student's performance (Farr & Beck, 1991). Interpreting the information is based on standards and criteria constructed not by outside agencies, as with formal practices, but by the teachers and students themselves. The focus of the evaluation is not only on the product but also on the process and performance (Worthen, 1993).

With the variety of approaches to alternative practices, it is important to consider whether the practice is sound in the construction and implementation.

Portfolios: An Approach to Alternative Assessment

In recent years, one form of alternative assessment has come to the forefront in discussions addressing assessment practices. Portfolios have been embraced by teachers of all grades as a method of evaluating students' performances that follow the four guiding principles outlined by Valencia. Paulson and Paulson (1991) offer a substantive definition of portfolio assessment:

> *A purposeful, integrated collection of student work showing student effort, progress, or achievement in one or more areas. The collection is guided by performance standards and includes evidence of students' self-reflection and participation in setting the focus, selecting contents, and judging merit. (p. 295)*

The portfolio concept is not new. Artists and craftsmen have been developing portfolios to display their talents and work for many years. Artists select pieces of work to reflect their talents and abilities. Those interested have an opportunity to view the artist and/or craftsman in many lights. The same concept has expanded to the educational setting. In the classroom, portfolios are constructed to represent a student's abilities in various areas. As collections of student performance and work, portfolios demonstrate to many that the learning process has taken place for individual students (Paulson & Paulson, 1991). With a portfolio as evidence of the learning process, it is possible to understand the path of growth and development a learner accomplishes over a certain period of time.

Recalling the first guiding principle, portfolio assessment practices are authentic in nature. Authentic refers to an activity that is meaningful to students and is fundamentally instructive as opposed to evaluative (Smith, 1994). Portfolios contain only artifacts, collected pieces of information, that are both meaningful and purposeful in displaying student progress in a myriad of contexts. The information gathered regarding student performance is used instructionally to guide curriculum and instruction, thereby meeting the students' needs. As an authentic assessment practice, portfolios attempt to assess the "orchestration, integration, and application of skills in meaningful contexts" (Valencia, 1990, p. 338).

With a portfolio as evidence of the learning process, it is possible to understand the path of growth and development a learner accomplishes over a certain period of time.

Secondly, portfolio assessment practices are on-going. Artifacts and sample work are collected and reflected upon throughout the instructional year. Portfolios offer evidence of growth and development as the pieces of information are evaluated. This process of collecting and assessing information is a continuous one as new artifacts are included and old pieces lose their relevance. Through the portfolios, learning is perceived as always evolving and changing.

The third guiding principle, assessing students on a multidimensional level, is evident in portfolio assessment practices. Because learning is complex and multifaceted, the assessment practices used to evaluate the learning should also be "committed to sampling a wide range of cognitive processes and affective responses" (Valencia, 1990, p. 338). Within the portfolio is a collection of work created in many contexts for a variety of purposes. Portfolios provide opportunities for students and teachers to better understand the expansive nature of learning and assessment.

And finally, collaborative reflection is an important aspect of portfolio assessment in that students and the teacher are both engaged in the evaluation process. The student is evaluating his/her own strengths and needs; the teacher is examining his/her own teaching effectiveness. Together, as partners in the assessment process, teachers and students actively engage in dialogue about learning and teaching. The collaborative reflection allows for new perspectives to emerge as students and teachers reach shared understandings about assessment and the value of portfolios in the process.

Portfolio By Any Other Name is Portfolio

Portfolios have received the attention of many in the educational community. With this attention, portfolios have been described as many things, from windows to the mind and telling a story, to containers of evidence and laboratories constructing meaning from experience (Fogan, 1989; Paulson & Paulson, 1991; Collins, 1992). Using metaphors to help explain portfolios provides the teacher and others with a context in which to understand the processes and functions involved. The visualizations created by these metaphors aid in clarifying some of the potential abstractness in assessing learning and knowledge. The window metaphor allows the teacher or other evaluator to see how something was created, and the telling a story metaphor provides the viewer with a sense that there is a progression of development—a beginning, middle, and an end in a student's learning process. The container of evidence creates an image of a concrete place in which information is stored to be used later to make evaluative decisions, while the laboratory metaphor encourages the student and teacher to view portfolios as a place where something, in this case knowledge, is created.

Just as a rose by any other name is a rose, portfolios by any other name have the same underlying goals and focus in understanding and documenting the learning process. Interpreting the various metaphors helps the teacher grasp the possibilities of portfolios. Portfolios are limited only by the imagination of the creator (Collins, 1992). So, whatever label is most comfortable and makes the most sense to you and your students is what should be utilized in your classroom.

Just as a rose by any other name is a rose, portfolios by any other name have the same underlying goals and focus in understanding and documenting the learning process.

Why Alternative Assessment, Especially Portfolios?

The last decade has brought with it a renewed interest in assessment practices throughout the grade levels. Support for this interest is at all levels of the educational system: classroom teachers, district personnel, and state officials. The reasons underlying a return to addressing various assessment practices teachers and students engage in come from three important areas of the educational process: philosophy of teaching and learning, linguistic and cultural diversity, and empowerment for teachers and students.

The ways in which learning and teaching occur in classrooms are being revisited by the educational community. Learning is viewed as a socially constructive process where "learners build their own knowledge structures rather than merely receive them from teachers" (Cooper, 1994, p.2). In many of today's classrooms, students are asked to solve problems utilizing their own backgrounds and experiences. This is quite different from earlier days where the student copied and memorized the answer provided by the teacher or textbook. Constructing knowledge is a social endeavor involving a "learning community"—student, teacher, peers, and others. The interactions among these participants as they engage in activities and tasks in a learning environment lead to new interpretations and meanings. As students construct their own knowledge and meanings, there is a movement away from a "transmission" model of teaching and learning, where teachers and textbooks provide knowledge, to a "process" model where students are active participants in creating meaningful understandings. To reflect the new perspectives of learning, teachers are beginning to incorporate a more authentic, higher-level thinking, performance-based curriculum. Instruction is more individualized, adaptive, and interactive (U.S. Congress, Office of Technology Assessment, 1992). This shift impacts not only the curriculum and instruction, but also influences assessment practices. Alternative assessment practices are attempting to accommodate this new perspective of learning. Recording and reporting student performance through portfolios, observational and anecdotal notes, hands-on activities, open-ended tasks, etc., reflects a constructivist perspective of learning and teaching.

To reflect the new perspectives of learning, teachers are beginning to incorporate a more authentic, higher-level thinking, performance-based curriculum.

Another cause impelling assessment practices to the forefront of current discussions is the increase of cultural and linguistic diversity among students in the classroom. The reliance of standardized assessment scores to influence the decisions made regarding instructional programs has not taken into account issues facing students of other cultures and other languages. Research on second language learning has reported that the issue of time is problematic in that the students spend so much time figuring out the language that they do not have time to answer the questions (Chamot, 1980; Garcia, 1991). Additionally, differences in cultural knowledge and interactional styles affect performance on standardized tests and ultimately academic achievement (Au & Jordon, 1982). Knowing the concerns raised by formal, standardized assessment practices for linguistically and culturally diverse students, teachers are beginning to implement alternative practices that better meet these students' needs. Alternative assessment practices provide teachers and students with possibilities to display knowledge in a variety of ways.

Along with the new views of learning and the diversity of students in today's classrooms, empowerment issues for teachers and students have entered the discussion on assessment practices. Traditional assessment practices do not provide teachers and students with opportunities to feel empowered about the decisions being rendered as a result of the assessment practices. With the social constructivist perspective of learning, knowledge is now being shared among the learning and teaching community. Alternative assessment practices are opening up the decision making process to all interested parties. Decisions about what is being assessed, how it will be evaluated, and why it is being assessed are now in teachers' and students' hands. This expanding notion of learning and assessment affords teachers and students opportunities to participate in assessment decisions and to feel part of the process, all of which leads to empowerment. In sharing the responsibility of assessment, teachers and students gain a sense of control over instruction, the curriculum and, ultimately, the academic program.

Three important reasons assessment issues have surfaced in recent educational discussions include alignment of philosophies in learning and assessment, linguistic and cultural diversity, and empowerment. The interest in alternative assessment practices in meeting the needs of both teachers and students will continue to increase as the educational community begins to acknowledge and address these significant issues. As teachers and students begin to utilize and discuss alternative assessment practices, the decisions made will be reflective of the instructional practices and of the meaningful activities students engage in throughout the learning process.

Alternative assessment practices are opening up the decision making process to all interested parties.

Settings that Support Alternative Assessment

Alternative assessment practices have risen from a revisited perspective of learning and teaching. Classroom settings that embrace a shared authority perspective, engage in meaningful and integrated instruction, and view assessment and instruction as a recurring process, each one driving the other, will find alternative assessment practices to meet the needs of the students and of the teacher. Sharing the authority in determining what knowledge and interpretations are accepted offers opportunities for new perspectives and interpretations to emerge (Ruddell & Unrau, 1994). As teachers release some of their control, students begin to contribute to the assessment process. Dialogues and conversations begin. Through dialogue, a more collaborative setting is established. Teachers and students, together, discuss and implement decisions regarding the instructional program and assessment practices. Opening up the decision making process to the learning community encourages multiple perspectives and interpretations to flourish. Sharing the authority promotes better understanding of learning and assessment. With a shift in authority to incorporate multiple interpretations, new meanings about learning are shaped and reshaped.

Classroom settings that provide for an integrated curriculum have in place an emphasis on learning rather than teaching, with learning perceived as a socially constructed experience. An integrated curriculum promotes authenticity by incorporating many skills and tasks into project oriented, collaborative activities, often revolving around a specified theme. A unit, for example, on the life cycle of a butterfly might incorporate many math activities on the length of each phase of a caterpillar's transformation to a butterfly. The mathematical component in determining number of days can be approached through a writing task of creating a biography of the life of a butterfly. Integrated curriculums foster alternative assessment practices. Skills are not assessed in a discrete, decontextualized manner but rather in an integrated, process oriented approach. A teacher may observe the students as they complete the task, place their work samples in portfolios, or have students reflect on the activity to determine understandings.

Classroom settings that provide for an integrated curriculum have in place an emphasis on learning rather than teaching, with learning perceived as a socially constructed experience.

And thirdly, assessment and instructional practices should be viewed as a recurring process whereby one influences and impacts the other. Classrooms that promote the integration of the two will provide teachers and students with knowledge about performance, as well as knowledge of future activities. The rich information gathered during meaningful instructional activities requires that it be interpreted in light of the next step to be taken in instruction. Alternative assessment practices enable teachers and students to make the connections between instruction and assessment. With the gathering of information over time and in a variety of contexts, it is possible to make informed decisions as to the appropriate instructional path to take to meet the needs of students.

Concluding Remarks

While reading and reflecting on the following chapters about portfolios and the possibilities presented for you and your students, it is important to remember that portfolios are a dynamic process. As windows, containers, or stories, portfolios offer glimpses into the thinking and learning of your students and of yourself as a teacher. "They represent a philosophy that honors both the process and the products of learning as well as the active participation of the teacher and the students in their own evaluation and growth" (Valencia, 1990, p. 340).

Moving From a Collection to Authentic Assessment

Documenting Progress

Portfolios are more than collections of students' work in folders to be reflected upon only during special events such as Open House and parent conferences. As an assessment practice, the purpose of a portfolio is not to store individual pieces of work but to document the growth and development of a student's learning process within an instructional program. Portfolios offer opportunities for the educational community: teachers, students, parents, district personnel, and other interested parties, to view the intersection between instruction and assessment (Paulson, Paulson, & Meyer, 1991). With a portfolio as evidence of the student's learning process, it is possible to construct a portrait, "one that a teacher and a student can learn from long after the isolated moment of assessment" (Wolf, 1989, p. 39).

As an assessment practice, the purpose of a portfolio is not to store individual pieces of work but to document the growth and development of a student's learning process within an instructional program.

The construction of meaningful and purposeful portfolio assessment based on five underlying elements. These elements are not evident in the individual artifacts collected by you or your student but are reflected in authentic uses of portfolios to integrate instruction and assessment. The elements include (1) collaboration, (2) an expanded view of learning and knowledge, (3) a place to view process, (4) exploration of multiple perspectives, and (5) reflection and self-assessment. The inclusion of these elements in portfolio assessment practices promotes opportunities for embracing the achievements, experiences, goals, and interests of engaged students in your classroom.

Collaboration: What Teachers and Students Share

Portfolios constructed through a collaborative effort between the student and teacher are meaningful to both parties. Collaboration occurs in decisions regarding goals and purposes, standards, contents, and the motivations behind the selected works. While goals, standards, and contents of portfolios are introduced in this section on collaboration, they will be expanded and further developed in greater detail in following chapters. Collaboration in the construction of a portfolio for authentic assessment purposes encourages students to participate and have a voice in the process, thereby advocating ownership of learning and thinking.

The key to authentic and effective use of portfolio assessment is to determine the purpose.

The first step in the collaborative process is establishing the goals and purposes for the portfolio. The key to authentic and effective use of portfolio assessment is to determine the purpose. The purpose should be constructed collaboratively to meet the needs of both you and your students. Understanding what each member of this collaborative team is expecting from the portfolio will provide clarity for the purposes of the portfolio. Sample questions to include when discussing portfolio goals with your students follow.

- Why do you want to participate in creating a portfolio?
- How will the portfolio help you as a student and me as a teacher?
- What will the portfolio be used for?
- What will be included in the portfolio?
- How much information are we going to collect for the portfolio?
- How are we going to evaluate the portfolio?
- What criteria is going to be established?

In addition to goals and purposes, standards for portfolios are also constructed collaboratively, depending on the interests and needs of the teacher and the student. Standards are based on what is valued by the teacher and the student and should be aligned with the established goals and purposes. Discussions between you and your student will determine how the portfolio is going to be evaluated. The selected pieces of work to be judged and the criteria by which they are to be judged are two important considerations to discuss with your students.

When thinking about standards, rubrics are often created to set a scoring guide. Rubrics are stated criteria on an articulated scale enabling an evaluator, usually the teacher, to differentiate among a group of student samples (Jasmine, 1993). For example, rubrics in writing might be on a scale from one to four.

- 1: No response—it was not included in the portfolio.

- 2: Writer does not have fluency in writing—the reader is unable to understand the ideas of the writer; lack of or inappropriate use of punctuation and capitalization; does not demonstrate use of descriptive language.

- 3: Writer demonstrates limited fluency in writing; appropriate use of punctuation and capitalization in most cases; limited use of descriptive language.

- 4: Student writes with fluency of ideas; includes appropriate punctuation and capitalization; uses descriptive language throughout the writing piece.

If your students are involved in deciding what is important and valued, the evaluation becomes more meaningful upon engagement in and reflection on the task.

In defining standards and rubrics collaboratively, both the student and the teacher become connected to the assessment process. If your students are involved in deciding what is important and valued, the evaluation becomes more meaningful upon engagement in and reflection on the task. For you, understanding what your students think is important will aid in your own teaching process. Standards, when constructed collaboratively, provide opportunities for students and teachers to better understand the learning process and what activities and steps, when taken together, encourage thoughtful, meaningful learning.

After the goals and standards are defined by the teacher and the student, collaboration continues as students select and collect pieces of work. During discussions on an individual basis with your students, you may engage in such questions as these.

- Why is this piece important to you?
- What does this piece of work show in terms of your growth as a writer, thinker, reader, etc.?
- What will be the next piece you include?

As your students respond to questions such as these while you provide some of your own input and suggestions to the construction of the portfolio, the collaborative atmosphere is maintained. Tied to the collection of materials is the motivation of the student and teacher to include certain pieces. A clear understanding of why pieces were selected to represent the growth and learning of a student enables you and your student to effectively use the portfolio for assessment as well as for future learning.

Collaboration, therefore, on all levels, is an important and critical piece of the portfolio assessment practice. The collaboration between teachers and students, from the goals and purposes to standards and evaluation, leads to a better understanding of the instructional process. Through the collaborative nature of portfolio assessment, teachers and students engage in dialogue about what is valued in our educational process and what steps or actions can be taken to promote academic achievement. Providing opportunities for you and your students to participate and have your voices heard gives credibility to the entire portfolio assessment practice. Collaboration is an inherent characteristic of authentic, meaningful assessment.

Knowledge and academic achievement are no longer perceived as the ability to correctly select one answer on a multiple-choice test, but, rather, knowledge is being assessed in many contexts.

Expanded View of Learning and Knowledge

Portfolio assessment practices offer a way for teachers and students to begin understanding the complex and multifaceted process of learning. Documentation and reflection on a variety of students' work created in diverse contexts and including other information gathered by the teacher allow viewing the learning process and knowledge acquisition through expanded lenses. Knowledge and academic achievement are no longer perceived as the ability to correctly select one answer on a multiple-choice test, but, rather, knowledge is being assessed in many contexts. Portfolios, as a method of alternative assessment practices, provide opportunities for the learning process to be documented and validated. Teachers and students are able to make connections between the actual knowledge gained and the processes involved.

The expanded view of what is validated and important in the learning process encourages teachers and students to explore new possibilities in the learning process. Portfolio assessment practices enable the parameters of learning to be pushed to the limit. A broader context for what is learned creates increased potential for students. Acknowledging that students learn material through varied approaches supports the use of portfolio assessment. Portfolios enable students to demonstrate the ways in which the learning process occurred through multiple samples in multiple contexts.

Additionally, portfolio assessment practices encourage diversity and complexity in thinking and learning. Students are able to come to tasks and activities knowing that their approaches to the situations will be validated and supported. Students bring to the activity their own background knowledge and experiences which impact how they proceed in new learning situations. Take, for example, an activity requiring second grade students to create a recipe for a meal for a literary character. Depending on the choice of literary character and the students' own experiences with recipes, there will be many ways to accomplish the task. Some students may write out recipes they already know. Others will research the eating habits of the character (i.e., what caterpillars eat) to create recipes. Some may be more interested in the availability and cost of ingredients needed to make the recipes. And still others may actually prepare recipes. The alternative approaches to the task are reflective of the varying backgrounds and experiences students bring to the classroom.

There is no single set of procedures or methods that guarantees achievement and knowledge acquisition for all students. Documenting how each student approaches tasks and activities will enable you to have a clearer picture as to how your students are thinking. Do the students understand the intricacies of recipes and measurement? What about eating habits? Do students appear to succeed in tasks maximizing one modality over the others? Did students have sufficient time to complete the task? As teachers and students expand their views of learning and teaching, the assessment practices will follow. What thinking did the students do? In what ways are you going to assess the learning? No two students are alike in their learning experiences. Expanding views of learning to include activities where evaluation is more than a paper and pencil routine is what alternative assessments are based on. Because the learning process is not the same for each student, the assessment practices should also reflect this diversity. Portfolios promote the expanded views of learning and teaching by incorporating many samples of work with different orientations into the portfolio.

Because the learning process is not the same for each student, the assessment practices should also reflect this diversity.

A Place to View Process

An important element of portfolio assessment practices is the documentation of the learning process that occurs for students in your classroom. The term process, in the context of assessment refers to the intermediate steps, including strategies, decisions, rough drafts, etc., the student takes in reaching the final or end product (Wiggins, 1989). The learning process is not approached the same way by all of your students. Some will make continuous progress towards established goals, others will appear to go in spurts, while never being confident that they will arrive at the determined goals. The significance of documenting students' learning processes is to authentically and effectively evaluate the actual learning that is occurring for your students. Understanding the processes your students participate in helps the weaving and constructing of their knowledge structures. The portfolio also enables students to grasp the notion that learning is not a one-shot, single snapshot activity but rather a dynamic, interactive, ongoing process. Learning is acquired over time. It is important for students, teachers, and parents to recognize the growth and development occurring over the course of an instructional year.

In collecting and reflecting upon student work throughout the year, it is possible to document the unfolding of students' learning over time and in a variety of contexts. Portfolio assessment practices enable those involved in the learning process to view the whole picture of the emerging student. "Portfolios provide insight into the range of different processes students can command or fail to grasp" (Wolf, 1987). With access to the selected pieces of work and the reflections on those pieces, you and your students gain better understandings of how learning is a process, involving steps to a determined goal, rather than a compilation of decontextualized, isolated products. Portfolios offer the possibility of seeing where your students excel and/or flounder and how learning shifts and advances over time.

The portfolio also enables students to grasp the notion that learning is not a one-shot, single snapshot activity but rather a dynamic, interactive, ongoing process.

Exploration of Multiple Perspectives

As an alternative assessment practice, portfolios encourage students and teachers to value and explore multiple perspectives of learning, thinking, and teaching. Viewing the multitude of processes in which students engage to construct meaning, it is possible to "imagine the worlds of others; to understand what it is like to stand in someone else's shoes" (Johnston, 1993, p. 429).

Portfolios are assembled in many different ways. Students come to the learning process with their own perspectives and backgrounds. Even with the same underlying purposes and goals established in a classroom, the students' portfolios will be individualized and unique. Different pieces of work and the reasons for those selections will vary from student to student. For instance, you may have one student who wants to include the activities enjoyed most, another may want to include only those that represent a finished product, and another may want only samples of writing in the portfolio. The diversity of artifacts within the portfolios encourages students and teachers to explore the many ways knowledge may be constructed.

Opportunities to share portfolios with peers and with you will expand perspectives on learning and thinking. Portfolios enable students and teachers to construct meaningful dialogues about the purposes and ways in which the collections were constructed. As the dialogues occur, it becomes evident that there are many approaches to learning and thinking. In sharing portfolios and understanding the perspectives and interpretations of others, portfolios promote the ability to imagine what went into the thinking process of your students and the production of the portfolios.

Acknowledging and expanding on the multiple perspectives brought forward through portfolios, enables teachers to reflect on their own approach towards teaching. Portfolio assessment practices encourage you to broaden your own perspectives about how learning occurs. As students select and validate their pieces of work in the various portfolios, you are provided the opportunity to better understand the ways in which learning occurs on an individual level. With the expanded view of the learning process, as it is reflected in the student portfolios, you are able to define and address the instructional needs of your students.

While the previous four elements are at the heart of portfolio assessment practices, reflection is the soul.

Reflection and Self-Assessment

While the previous four elements are at the heart of portfolio assessment practices, reflection is the soul. Reflection provides opportunities to critically examine the experiences and products of the portfolio, as well as the interpretations of those experiences (Graham, 1993). Portfolios encourage teachers and students to reflect upon those very experiences and activities that are located within the collection. As members of the learning community, students' reflections enable teachers and students to better understand and gain perspectives on the learning process. Reflection enables teachers to plan and direct their activities with foresight (Goodman, 1991).

Reflection practices often occur on an informal level for teachers. Many of you reflect on an unconscious level as you plan units of study and activities that are appropriate for your students. Questions considered may include:

- How did my students do on the last activity involving problem solving?
- What were the reactions of my students when they had the opportunity to select their own work partners?
- Did the teams work well together?
- I realize that my students did not grasp the concept—what approach did I use, and what will I try next?

These questions, while very important, are frequently not addressed on a formal level. Rarely do teachers verbalize or write down their reflections. Additionally, these reflective comments are not often shared with students and other colleagues.

Many teachers implementing portfolio assessment practices in their classrooms have either not included reflection as an aspect of the portfolio, or if students are reflecting on their work and decisions there has been little modeling of the process. If the element of reflection is left out, the portfolio becomes nothing more than a haphazard collection of work. Recall that assessment means trying to find the best match between a student and the learning environment; without some aspect of reflection occurring on a conscious level, this match is almost impossible to find. On the other hand, for students who are being asked to reflect on various pieces of work without modeling from the teacher, the reflections are often at a surface level, written or verbalized for the teacher, not for the student.

Recall that assessment means trying to find the best match between a student and the learning environment; without some aspect of reflection occurring on a conscious level, this match is almost impossible to find.

So, how does the soul of portfolio assessment go from the internal, informal thoughts of teachers and students to the verbalized, explicit thinking that is necessary to gain understandings and perspectives? To begin with, it is important to define two types of reflection: reflection-in-action and reflection-on-action (Graham, 1993). Reflection-in-action occurs during the course of the activity and is on an implicit, intuitive level. It is framed in the context in which the activity is occurring. As teachers and students engage in reflection-in-action practices, taken into consideration are such things as what the prior background and experiences are; whether there is a common understanding of the purpose of the activity; and the appropriateness of the activity. Reflection-in-action contributes to the possible choices of actions taken during an activity.

For example, a group of third grade students are engaged in writing about the character motivation of Charlotte, the spider, in the classic story of *Charlotte's Web* (White, 1952). As the activity progresses, the teacher notices a few students with quizzical looks on their faces. At this point, the teacher and these students make an intuitive, reflection-in-action decision. The teacher may alter the course of the activity and provide opportunities to further discuss why Charlotte responded the way she did. This change in the course of the activity enables the students to gain a better understanding of character motivation and, therefore, write a strong and effective piece. Reflection-in-action practices encourage teachers and students to constantly revise and revisit the initial purposes of the activity.

Relating reflection-in-action practices to portfolio assessment, it is possible to alter the course of the assessment practice as teachers and students develop the portfolios. Portfolios are flexible and dynamic, limited only by the imagination and desires of those constructing them. The goals and purposes initially established may not be the ones to be highlighted later on. This change occurring during the assessment activity is an example of reflection-in-action. As the students and teachers revisit the goals and purposes of portfolios, new pieces of work demonstrating other aspects of the learning process might be collected, therefore altering the course of the activity. With the possibilities and potential portfolio assessment practices offer, reflection-in-action should be a critical aspect of reflection throughout the entire assessment process.

Portfolios are flexible and dynamic, limited only by the imagination and desires of those constructing them.

Reflection-on-action is what many are familiar with when discussing reflection. This reflective process occurs after the activity has been completed and is on an explicit level. "This type of reflection is usually more focused since attention is directed at examining the activity and is not diverted by the multiple demands of the situation" (Graham, 1993, p. 23). Reflection-on-action encourages teachers and students to look at activities and determine the worthiness and effectiveness of such activities.

Recalling the scenario about character motivation and writing, reflection-on-action practices occur after the students have completed the writing task. Considering the activity, the teacher may question whether the students gained a better understanding of character motivation and how to write effectively and clearly. The methods used to introduce and teach this concept will also be reflected upon. Students are asked such questions as What was learned in this activity? or What did you like/dislike about the activity? or What would you change for next time?

Reflection-on-action practices in portfolio assessment are evident in the reflective statements that students write regarding the pieces of work selected to represent their growth and development. These reflective statements contain such information as why those particular pieces were included, what was gained in the process of the activities, and how those pieces represent their learning processes.

Reflection-on-action is not intuitive like reflection-in-action. Rather it requires explicit action to be taken, acknowledging the multifaceted, complex learning process. It is a process that must be modeled and developed over time. Even teachers, as adults and as professionals, often express difficulty in verbalizing their own reflective thoughts to colleagues and others in the educational community.

The same is true for students. It takes practice for both students and teachers to go from "I like this piece of writing, because I like the topic" and "Teaching this unit was exciting because the students enjoyed the activities" to "This piece of writing shows that by using descriptive phrases I am able to create pictures with my words" and "The activities in this unit reflect my use of multiple pathways to learning. All three modalities are utilized as I attempt to engage the students in the learning process."

Learning to engage in reflective thinking is not an easy process. It can be encouraged and practiced through the use of prompts and reflection forms. Forms and prompts such as those found on the next few pages provide examples of what might be included when engaging your students in reflective activities. These prompts are content area specific, Language Arts, but can be modified for any subject area. When the form is completed, attach it to the work and include it in the student's portfolio. The last student prompt, however, is asking students to examine not just one writing activity but a collection of writings, and to reflect on their growth and development.

As teachers reflect on their own teaching practices, the possibilities to engage students in meaningful learning activities increase.

Teacher reflection forms can serve the same initial purposes as those for students. The prompts provide teachers with a place to start when making the leap from internal, informal reflections to explicit statements about their own growth as teachers. As teachers reflect on their own teaching practices, the possibilities to engage students in meaningful learning activities increase. An example of a teacher reflection prompt is provided on page 21. Again, the prompts can be altered to best meet your needs as you reflect on your teaching practices.

Reflections on Writing
Primary Form

Name ______________________ Date __________________

When I look back at the work I have done, I feel

☺ 😐 ☹

I have gotten better in writing sentences.

using capitals and periods.

spelling.

telling a story.

telling my ideas about something.

I am really proud of

____

Next time I write I will

____

Reprinted from TCM504 Portfolios and Other Assessments, *Teacher Created Materials, 1993*

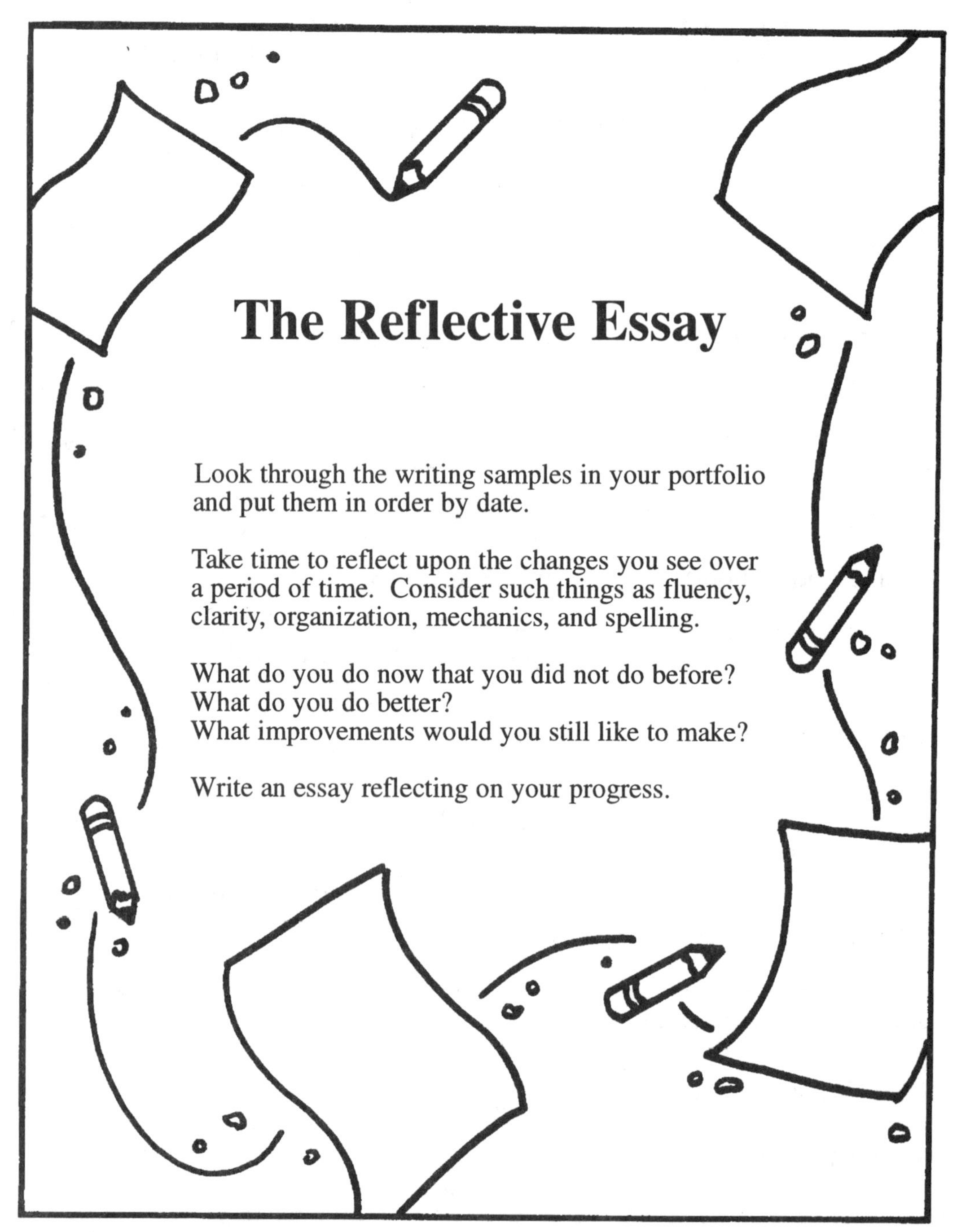

Reprinted from TCM504 Portfolios and Other Assessments, *Teacher Created Materials, 1993*

Teacher Reflection

My intentions and goals for this activity were to have my students

____

____

____

I think that my students were able to ____________________

____

____

____

My students were engaged and interested during ____________

____

____

____

My students lost focus or were confused during ____________

____

____

____

Suggestions for future activities ______________________

____

____

Additional comments ____________________________

____

____

Reflection-in-action and reflection-on-action practices are part of portfolio assessment practices in all grades. Beginning in the primary grades, students can reflect, verbally or in writing, on what they have learned and how they went about it. As students progress into the upper grades, reflective thinking should become a natural extension of their learning. The reflective thinking you engage in as a teacher will improve your teaching practices as you better meet the needs of your students. Reflection, therefore, is an integral aspect of portfolio assessment practices.

Concluding Remarks

The five elements of collaboration, expanded view of learning, importance of process, multiple perspectives, and reflection are essential to the success of portfolio assessment practices. These elements provide teachers and students with opportunities to engage in the learning and assessment processes. Collaboration and reflection encourage ownership and voice in the processes. The expanded views of learning, multiple perspectives, and the importance of process enable the diversities and complexities of learning and teaching to be recognized. With these five elements incorporated and ingrained into portfolios, teachers and students will benefit from the "complete" picture portfolio assessment practices offer.

Guidelines for Portfolio Assessment Practices

Guidelines as a Framework

Portfolio assessment practices serve a variety of purposes and are unique and individual to the creators (students) and to the evaluators (teachers). With the diversity of portfolios, there are no established and set rules or steps to be taken to insure success with the practice. Portfolios are not easy. In fact, they are messy and involve work. Messy, in this case, refers to the unclear, unstructured, gray area of assessment. Portfolios are not as simple as giving a paper and pencil test with predetermined answers and scoring. Portfolios do not come with set standards, criteria, and ways to evaluate as do standardized testing practices. So what do you do? How does one begin to utilize portfolios in the classroom? How do portfolios go from a folder to an authentic assessment practice?

Portfolios are not easy. In fact, they are messy and involve work.

To make the transition an easy and effective process, there are guidelines that you can begin to follow. These guidelines include (1) defining the purpose of the portfolio, (2) defining the audience who will judge and evaluate the contents of the portfolio, and (3) establishing the standards and criteria by which the contents will be judged. The guidelines provide a framework in which to develop your own uses of portfolios. Defining the purpose, audience, and standards are, perhaps, the three most critical steps in moving folders containing work samples towards authentic assessment practices.

Purposes: More Than a Storehouse of Work

The purposes of portfolios, as discussed in the previous chapter, are multifaceted. Initially, for many teachers portfolios are introduced into their thinking and practice as a way to document the growth of students' learning. Through portfolio assessment practices, teachers and students are able to follow the development of skills and abilities over time. Rather than recording scores or grades on isolated activities and tasks, portfolios enable you and your students to see how changes and developments occur over a period of time. Portfolios, then, become "representatives of all of the processes and products involved in the students' learning process" (Jongsma, 1989, p. 264).

Ownership and decision making are important aspects to developing students who are autonomous learners.

While documenting growth and development of students' learning processes is an important and valid use of portfolios, there are additional purposes portfolios serve. One of these purposes is to encourage student ownership and decision making. Ownership and decision making are important aspects to developing students who are autonomous learners. Ownership of the learning process is achieved as students are involved in making decisions regarding the purposes for the portfolios, the materials to be placed in the portfolios, and the ways in which the portfolios will be evaluated. For the teacher, portfolios provide a focal point to engage students in discussions about learning, process, and activities. With time, experience, and conversations, students' abilities to understand and discuss their own learning process deepens. As a purpose identified in the establishment of portfolios, student ownership and decision making are realized through collaboration between teachers and students.

Another purpose of portfolio assessment practice is to provide an opportunity for reflection regarding instructional practice and to possibly influence curriculum decisions. Teachers using portfolios in their classrooms can use information gathered for a variety of purposes, "the primary of which is to plan instructional experiences for children" (Heibert, 1991, p. 511). With the documentation available in your students' portfolios about how they accomplished various tasks and activities and the processes in which they engaged in, you can make an informed decision as to the most appropriate instructional path to travel. For example, by viewing how your students worked through a series of open-ended math problems over a two month period, you will be able to determine whether or not their understanding of mathematical concepts and thinking patterns have developed. Additionally, through the collaborative reflection between you and your students, you will hear their voices and interests. This, too, impacts the instructional decisions you make regarding the academic program for your students. The rich information provided both in the process of creating portfolios and in the portfolios themselves enables teachers to gain new views of their accomplishments in teaching (Wolf, 1989). Through portfolios you will be able to determine what aspects of your instructional program are effective and meaningful for your students.

The differing purposes for engaging in portfolio assessment practices do not have to stand alone. It is feasible and possible for teachers and students to have all three of these purposes and perhaps more. Teachers should utilize the information provided in the portfolios to guide and drive their instructional decisions as well as document the growth of their students. Students, in addition to being interested in viewing their own growth and development, are also interested in having the portfolios provide opportunities for decision making strategies and ownership of the learning process. Portfolios, therefore, serve many purposes for students, teachers, and interested others.

Teachers should utilize the information provided in the portfolios to guide and drive their instructional decisions as well as document the growth of their students.

However, what is important to keep in mind is that the purposes for establishing a portfolio system in your classroom should be defined before the process begins. Refer to the questions in chapter two on collaborative purpose setting; you can address these as you and your students determine the goals for the portfolios. What do you want the portfolios to achieve? Is it to determine what instructional practices are most effective? Or, is it to evaluate your students utilizing a method that "paints" a more complete picture of their learning processes in a variety of contexts? Regardless of the reasons you and your students are engaging in creating portfolios, defining the specific purposes and goals is a critical step in effective and meaningful assessment.

Audience: Who is interested?

In connection with the purpose of implementing portfolios in your classroom, the guideline of audience is one that is often not taken into consideration. Yet, audience plays a significant role in determining the effectiveness and success of portfolio assessment in the classroom. Just as there are different purposes and goals for portfolios, there are also different audiences looking at various aspects of the portfolio. The audience refers to those individuals or groups who are using the contents of a portfolio, to evaluate or understand the thinking patterns of the creator of the portfolio.

The first most obvious audience is the teacher. What information does the teacher hope to gain from viewing the collected contents of the portfolio? This is where the audience is connected to the purpose. Depending on the intentions of the teacher, the contents in the portfolio have different implications. For example, if a teacher is interested in evaluating a student's ability to write events in chronological order and use interesting language, the selected pieces of work demonstrating this task will be of importance. The teacher, on the other hand, may be using the portfolio to document the instructional activities that appeared to be effective in developing competent writers. With this in mind, the pieces of work that the student appeared to complete successfully and the thinking process that went into its completion are going to be looked at. The purpose defined by the audience, in this case the teacher, directly affects how the contents of the portfolio are going to be viewed.

The contents in a portfolio are more telling than a single abstract grade with teacher explanation.

The creator of the portfolio, your student, also plays the role of the audience. As an audience member, your student will view his/her own portfolio with great interest. What information is revealed about him/herself as a learner? Just as with you, the purposes of the portfolio will impact your student's perspective on his/her achievements in the learning process. The student, as the audience, will reflect on the choices and decisions made in the portfolio. With this information , your student will gain new understandings as to his/her own strengths and weaknesses in various areas. These understandings have implications for future activities. How the student perceives him/herself is carried on into new activities. The portfolio, therefore, becomes important to your student in serving as a springboard to develop worthwhile personal academic goals. The dual role the student plays in creating and evaluating the portfolio is significant for the success of portfolio assessment practices.

Who else might express interest in the contents of the portfolios? Those outside the classroom have a vested interest in the portfolios. Parents, other teachers, principles, and district and state personnel are audiences that will view the portfolios with different perspectives. Parents are interested in knowing how well their own child is performing. Through portfolios and jointly constructed conferences, parents are able to understand their child's progress more completely. The contents in a portfolio are more telling than a single abstract grade with teacher explanation. While this is a benefit of portfolios, it is important to remember that parents may be unaccustomed to the new perspectives of learning and assessment practices. With this in mind, it is critical to invest some time early in the year explaining and discussing with parents what purposes the portfolios serve and how the collected samples demonstrate those purposes. For example, a portfolio with first draft pieces of work or idea pieces not subjected to corrections may cause the parent to think you are not properly grading the work and become concerned about your teaching methods. As parents become comfortable with portfolios as an assessment practice, they will be able to offer their own perspectives and interpretations, thereby adding to the richness of the portfolio.

Other teachers have their own perspectives of the portfolios constructed by students. Future teachers may be using the portfolios as an initial evaluation of the strengths and talents of students as they enter their classrooms at the beginning of the instructional year. They may view portfolios as more detailed pictures of the skills and concepts achieved by students. Perusing the portfolios constructed by their new students, prospective teachers are able to develop an initial curriculum that will meet the needs and interests of the students.

Perusing the portfolios constructed by their new students, prospective teachers are able to develop an initial curriculum that will meet the needs and interests of the students.

On the other hand, district and state personnel have their own perspectives and uses for the contents in portfolios. This group, as an audience of portfolios, is not connected to the individual student and her/his portfolio but rather to large groups of students' performances. Therefore, the reasons and goals they have in mind while evaluating portfolios are broader in nature. District and state personnel are often interested in the success of curriculum and programs for various schools. Issues of standardization and accountability are also of concern. How does this affect you and your students as portfolios are constructed? The contents included in portfolios for large scale assessment practices may emphasize standard formats and routines. Your students might have to include something that is standardized for all students in your particular grade. The inclusion of formatted pieces of work will alter the true authenticity of the portfolio but will serve the desired purposes of the district and state.

The audiences for portfolio assessment practices bring to the process varied and differing perspectives. Everyone views and assesses the portfolio with a different set of glasses, a personal frame of reference, and an individually held value system (Paulson & Paulson, 1991). Whether the interest is in reflecting on instructional practice, documenting growth, or determining curricular programs, student portfolios have the potential to meet the needs of all audiences. The unique and divergent intentions of the audiences will impact the contents of the portfolios. Therefore, knowing the audience and the perspective being brought into the evaluation process is of significance in the construction and success of portfolios in your classroom.

Standards and Criteria: How are They Established?

Evaluating portfolios is the third critical guideline in developing a successful and meaningful portfolio assessment practice. It is also the most difficult. Because portfolios are constructed with individual students in mind and for a variety of purposes and audiences, there are no guarantees, nationally normed scores, or grade level equivalents to refer to (Wolf, LeMahieu, & Erish, 1992). Evaluators are being asked to interpret the many pieces of information within a portfolio. The interpretations are often based on established criteria, rubrics, and standards. Constructing rubrics that are appropriate require not only knowledge of curriculum and instruction but also knowledge of assessment strategies (Valencia & Calfee, 1991). In addition, establishing and defining standards and rubrics are additional responsibilities most teachers do not have much experience in. Traditionally, standards and criteria are predetermined by outside sources at the district, state, and national level. Classroom teachers rarely have the opportunity to construct standards by which to evaluate their students. With the implementation of alternative assessment practices, however, this is changing. Teachers are now being asked to define and construct standards and rubrics but often with little practice or knowledge. The following section will help in providing some keys to establishing standards and criteria for portfolios in your classroom.

Both students and teachers should be clear as to the ways the portfolios are going to be evaluated.

Evaluation involves making sense of and using the information gathered (Biggam, 1994). The process of determining whether or not your students are meeting the established goals and purposes is decided by you and your students in a collaborative setting. Again, refer to chapter two and the collaboration that occurs in establishing standards and criteria for the portfolios. Both students and teachers should be clear as to the ways the portfolios are going to be evaluated. What is judged depends not only on the beliefs about what is important but also on how the information gained will be used (Paulson & Paulson, 1991).

To begin answering these questions about beliefs and importance of information, you and your students may engage in constructing a meaningful rubric system for your assessment practices. A rubric is an articulated set of criteria on a scale. It is a method of evaluating a student's work using defined criteria. Rubrics can be developed for any grade on any task. At each level of the rubric, from the highest to the lowest, words and phrases are used to describe the characteristics at each point on the scale. When evaluating a portfolio or selections of work within a portfolio through rubrics, teachers, students, parents, and other educators have more accurate understandings of what is expected for high-quality work. The words and phrases are quite descriptive, making the expectations explicit (Winograd, 1994).

In developing a rubric system, you and your students will clarify the skills and abilities that are expected at each level. Such documents as state curriculum frameworks, district frameworks, and curriculum guides will provide helpful guidelines when constructing an appropriate set of criteria. The criteria reflect what you believe to be the defining characteristics at each level. As your students participate in this process, be aware of their tendencies to set unrealistically high standards and requirements for themselves. With time and practice in rubric development, however, your students will begin to develop more realistic expectations and perspectives of their learning processes. In addition to defining the specific objectives, you will also determine how many levels you want to establish in the rubric system. This number usually ranges from three to six. Obviously, the more levels you include in your rubric system, the greater the subtleties in the defining characteristics (Jasmine, 1994).

The criteria reflect what you believe to be the defining characteristics at each level.

On the next few pages are examples of generalized and elaborate rubrics that can be implemented for any task within a portfolio. These samples of generalized rubrics can provide you with a framework from which you and your students can develop more specific and meaningful sets of criteria. The elaborate rubric is content specific, mathematics. Again these forms can be altered for any task in any content area.

Generalized Task Rubric

The generalized task rubric on this page is a 4-point rubric. The categories are broad. Scores 4 and 3 are high/average and Scores 2 and 1 indicate a need for more instruction. With this rubric, the papers can be quickly divided into two piles (high above the line, low below the line) and then given a specific score.

Generalized Task Rubric/4-point

Score 4: **Demonstrates Complete Understanding**
- ◆ Comprehends and uses mathematical ideas.
- ◆ Communicates thinking clearly.

Score 3: **Demonstrates Adequate Understanding**
- ◆ Uses and shows adequate comprehension of mathematical ideas.
- ◆ Communicates most of thinking process.

Score 2: **Demonstrates Limited Understanding**
- ◆ Shows limited comprehension in the use of mathematical ideas.
- ◆ Communication is incomplete or incorrect.

Score 1: **Demonstrates Little or No Understanding**
- ◆ Shows little or no comprehension and/or uses of mathematical ideas.
- ◆ Is not able to communicate mathematical ideas.

Reprinted from TCM506 Middle School Assessment, *Teacher Created Materials, 1994*

Elaborated Task Rubric for a Math Problem - Grade 3 or 4

Score 6: ***Exemplary Achievement***

- ◆ Demonstrates internalized understanding of major concepts.
  - Draws a spinner that clearly illustrates another way to show a fifty/fifty chance for red.
  - Writes a clear and accurate reason for his/her design and is able to discuss with a partner (group).
  - Creates additional spinners and labels them correctly.

Score 5: ***Commendable Achievement***

- ◆ Demonstrates detailed understanding of major concepts.
  - Draws a spinner that clearly illustrates another way to show a fifty/fifty chance for red.
  - Writes a clear and accurate reason for his/her design and is able to discuss with a partner (group).

Score 4: ***Adequate Achievement***

- ◆ Demonstrates a general understanding of the major concepts.
  - Draws a spinner that clearly illustrates another way to show a fifty/fifty chance for red.
  - Attempts to write or explain design orally but is only partially successful.

Score 3: ***Some Evidence of Achievement***

- ◆ Demonstrates a partial understanding of the major concepts.
  - Draws a correct spinner but makes no attempt to explain reasoning.

Score 2: ***Limited Evidence of Achievement***

- ◆ Demonstrates a lack of skills necessary to reach conclusion or solution.
  - Draws spinner or gives reasons that have little to do with the original problem.

Score 1: ***Minimal Evidence of Achievement***

- ◆ Demonstrates a lack of understanding.
  - Misinterprets problem or directions or both.

Score 0: ***No Response***

Reprinted from TCM504 Portfolios and Other Assessments, Teacher Created Materials, 1993

An important aspect to keep in mind as you engage in developing rubrics is that they are dynamic and should be revised as your expectations and your students' needs change. As you look at the distribution of scores in your students' work and portfolios, do you have too many high scores or no passing scores? Are the results consistent with the way you envision your class? Questions to consider include:

- Are your expectations high enough? Or too high?
- Did your students understand the directions?
- Did you require something that perhaps was not taught or explained?
- Did you want this particular result?

An important aspect to keep in mind as you engage in developing rubrics is that they are dynamic and should be revised as your expectations and your students' needs change.

Addressing these questions periodically as you and others evaluate the success of your rubric system will enable the system to be effective and meaningful.

Establishing standards and rubrics with your students promotes more responsive teaching and learning. Through the process of constructing rubrics, you become more aware of teaching strategies that are effective for your students. You gain a better understanding of your students' learning patterns and are better equipped to meet their needs. For your students, being engaged in the process of defining the expectations by which they are to be evaluated and judged provides power and ownership of learning.

In addition to evaluating the tasks within portfolios, teachers may also want to evaluate students' portfolios as a whole. A checklist of items to be located within the portfolio provides the students with an understanding of the expectations of the portfolio. For the teacher, the checklist offers a quick overview of the items in a student's portfolio. The checklist can be used to develop a set of scores to evaluate the portfolio. For example, a score of 4 indicates all identified items are accounted for, and the reflective statements were in depth. A score of 3 represents a complete portfolio, but the reflective statements do not provide insight into the thinking patterns of the student. A score of 2 or 1 indicates that the portfolio is not complete, either in artifacts to be included or in reflective statements. A sample checklist is included on the following page.

Portfolio Requirements for Language Arts

Student Name: ________________________________

Writing Samples (One writing sample for each month. Enter a date. List by title and type.)

__________ ____

__________ ____

__________ ____

__________ ____

__________ ____

__________ ____

__________ ____

Teacher/Student Conference Records (Enter dates.)

__________ __________ __________ __________

Other Student Requirements

____

____

Teacher Additions

____

____

Reprinted from TCM Workshop Notebook "Portfolios and Other Alternative Assessments", *Teacher Created Materials, 1993*

The process of constructing standards and rubrics is, therefore, essential when developing and implementing portfolio assessment practices. Rubrics enable students and teachers to have a clearer, more defined understanding of the ways in which learning and tasks are assessed. The checklists provide a method of accounting for the artifacts located in the portfolios. Rubrics and checklists remove from assessment practices the vagueness and abstractness of grades. By implementing rubrics and checklists in portfolio assessment practices, teachers and students are able to justify and validate their reasons for evaluating the selected pieces of work and the portfolio as a whole.

Concluding Remarks

As the three guidelines of purpose, audience, and standards come together to move portfolios from folders to an authentic assessment practice, what is important to remember is that each guideline influences the other two. What the purposes are will impact both the audience's perception of the portfolio and the way the portfolio is judged. The defined standards and rubrics have implications for the purposes of the portfolio, and the audience in turn impacts the standards and criteria established by the students and the teacher. The recurring, interactive nature of these guidelines creates a dynamic assessment practice. The challenge, then, in establishing a meaningful portfolio assessment practice is to provide opportunities for both yourself and your students to clearly articulate the reasons, intentions, and standards of the portfolio (Paulson & Paulson, 1991).

Types of Portfolios: From Showcase to Process

Four Types of Portfolios

Now that you are knowledgeable about the elements and guidelines underlying the construction of a meaningful portfolio to be used for assessment purposes, the next step is to familiarize yourself with the various types of portfolios. As stated earlier, portfolios serve many different purposes. The purpose for the portfolio will determine the types of materials and artifacts to be collected. "Depending on the tradition, the purpose, and the context, a portfolio may be evidence of one's own work, the work of others [in a cooperative group setting], solitary work, mentored work, best work, or all work" (Collins, 1992, p. 452). The materials collected in the portfolio will categorize the portfolio as one of four types. Valencia and Calfee (1991) have gathered research on portfolios and identified three types. The two most common in classroom are the showcase and documentation portfolios. Evaluation portfolios are usually outside the scope of classroom purposes. In later work, Valencia and Place (in press) identified a fourth type of student portfolio, the process portfolio. This portfolio demonstrates work that is part of a larger project.

The purpose for the portfolio will determine the types of materials and artifacts to be collected.

Showcase Portfolios

Showcase portfolios are the most common in classrooms implementing portfolio assessment practices. It is this type of portfolio that teachers are most often introduced to in in-service workshops and seminars. The showcase portfolio is just as the name implies. It is a collection of work the student and teacher believe to represent the student's best efforts. The selections chosen can range from one to many curricular subjects, depending on the desires of the student and teacher.

Typically, a showcase portfolio involves the student in making the decisions as to which pieces to include. "The unique feature of this type is that the student selects most of the entries, so that the portfolio emerges as a unique portrait of the individual over time" (Valencia & Calfee, 1991).

It is important that the decisions made regarding specific pieces of work are clearly articulated.

Suggested, however, is a collaborative effort between the student and teacher. Teachers and students come to the selection process with different perspectives. It is important that the decisions made regarding specific pieces of work are clearly articulated. The audience for showcase portfolios usually includes teachers, parents, and students. Encouraging discussions about the reasons why selections were made will promote clarity and understanding for the audience. Questions such as these may help promote discussions.

- Why did you select this piece of work for your portfolio?
- What will this piece tell someone about your learning and progress?
- What makes this piece of work your best?
- Can you tell me how this piece of work came to be your best? What steps did you take?

Answering these questions with your students will provide reflection and collaboration, both of which are important to the authenticity of the portfolio. In addition to discussions, written responses to the questions can also be included in the portfolio. Two samples of a general form you may want to use with your students are found on the next two pages. Written responses may be overwhelming when included with every piece of work. Use your own judgment to determine how often and when to engage your students in reflecting on their work.

MY BEST BECAUSE . . .

Name ________________________________ Date ______________

1. I picked this piece of work I completed in ________________ as my best because ____
____
____
____

2. As I worked on this task I tried to do the following steps to make it a "best" piece of work ____
____
____
____

3. This piece of work shows that I can now ______________________
____
____
____

4. The next time I complete a task like this one I will ______________
____
____
____

You might prefer, if you are teaching upper grades, to guide your students to write their responses in a reflective paragraph:

Name ______________________________ Date ________________

Why this is my best sample of . . .

In a paragraph or so, please write why this selection is representative of your best efforts in this discipline. Please include for the reader how this piece became your best, what criteria you used to determine its standing, what you have learned in completing the task, and how you might improve on your other selections to put them into the *best* category.

____

____

____

____

____

____

____

____

____

____

____

Limitations of the Showcase Portfolio

While the showcase portfolio is a wonderful opportunity for the student to exhibit strengths and talents, it also has limitations. One important limitation to recognize is the lack of process pieces in the portfolio. The evaluator views only the "best" work a student and/or teacher has selected. It is not possible for the evaluator to discern where the student started in the learning process and what growth was made. The evaluator is only able to determine what the student is capable of producing, not how the student went about producing the work. Access to only finished products, some with reflective statements, is a significant limitation of the showcase portfolic

A second limitation of the showcase portfolio is the difficulty in establishing standards and criteria to evaluate the portfolio. Each portfolio is a unique collection of work making it almost impossible to define any set standards. Determining how you and others are going to evaluate the "best" work of a student is a complex task. Are there degrees of excellence among your students? Additionally, how does a showcase portfolio fit into the grading scales that most teachers and districts are being asked to use? Or does it? A showcase portfolio as a method of evaluating students in the learning process is one that may require revisiting the standard format of grading practices. Many classrooms and districts are beginning to implement new formats in report cards, those with checklists and narratives rather than grades. Will this help in evaluating the showcase portfolio? Perhaps, but it is important to remember that the initial evaluation process is one that is complex. It will require looking beneath the surface of the items in the portfolio to determine what was gained in the process of constructing the portfolio.

Implementing showcase portfolio assessment practices in your classroom will allow your students to shine and display their many strengths and talents.

It is important to recognize these elements as limitations, not as impossible hurdles. As with any meaningful and effective assessment practice, it is a difficult process. Implementing showcase portfolio assessment practices in your classroom will allow your students to shine and display their many strengths and talents.

Documentation Portfolio

The documentation portfolio is the second most common type of portfolio used in classrooms throughout the country. This portfolio will have aspects of the showcase portfolio, but there are some distinctive differences. Just as the name "showcase" implies a specific collection of work, the label "documentation" means observing and recording progress in the learning process. Teachers have often informally created documentation portfolios to assess student growth for report cards and parent conference purposes. Teachers will gather a student's work throughout the year to justify and validate her/his learning and achievements. The collection, however, is not as systematic to measure growth and learning. A documentation portfolio enables teachers and students to collect work systematically and with defined purposes. Within the parameters of a documentation portfolio is a collection of work that over a specified time demonstrates the student's learning process. Again the collection can represent one or more curricular areas.

Included in the collection of work are rough drafts, brainstorming activities, various math tasks that demonstrate learning a process, checklists, observational notes recorded during activities, responses given in discussions, running records for reading tasks, etc. Virtually any piece of information that you and the student believe to be pertinent to documenting the learning process can be included in the portfolio. Because this portfolio often includes information developed by the teacher, you may have more input as to what goes into this type of portfolio than the showcase portfolio. But as noted earlier, a collaborative effort engages both parties to the fullest.

Virtually any piece of information that you and the student believe to be pertinent to documenting the learning process can be included in the portfolio.

To make the documentation portfolio more effective for assessing student growth, collecting a few selected pieces for each concept or idea learned will provide important evidence of the progress. For example, included in a documentation portfolio might be a first draft of an idea piece, a revision with peer editing comments, and a final draft. This way it is possible for the evaluator to see the learning patterns of the student. With the interest and purpose of the documentation portfolio to document growth and progress, it is not necessary to grade every piece of work. What is important is to evaluate the items in light of where the student began and where the student ended. Occasionally, a documentation portfolio is used in placement decisions for students, because it is representative of the work a student produces and the learning process.

As with the showcase portfolio, reflective discussions are critical to understanding the learning process of the students. Both you and your students should engage in reflecting on what growth was attained and the process involved. Using the reflection forms found on pages 19-21, or others you feel comfortable with, will provide a base from which to start the reflection process. Reflection is significant in the documentation portfolio because of the great emphasis placed on the learning process of students. The process is not explicit and needs to be brought forth through reflection. Again, it is not necessary or even possible to reflect on every item in the portfolio. Use your own judgment to decide which items to reflect on, both for yourself and your students.

Limitations of the Documentation Portfolio

Limitations of a documentation portfolio include the time involved and knowing what to do with all the collected samples and information. Documentation portfolios are somewhat time consuming. This is a significant limitation in that most teachers do not have additional time in their busy daily schedules. The time involved in implementing documentation portfolios is the systematic recording and storing of students' behavior and progress. Contributing information on a regular basis to students' portfolios is not an automatic task for many teachers, and it takes practice. There are some techniques, however, to reduce the amount of time it takes to record students' behavior and progress. Utilizing such methods as jotting information on "sticky notes" to be then placed in the portfolio for later reference and reflection, clipboards with checklists and places to record quick anecdotal notes, and encouraging students to discuss their own learning as you listen will help in effectively using your time.

The limitations are not meant to prevent you from engaging in portfolio assessment.

The information you and your students collect for the portfolios is extensive. With documentation portfolios, the limitation comes in having large amounts of information and knowing how to evaluate the various pieces. Over a given amount of time, usually six to eight weeks, students can accumulate quite a bit of important information. Think about the amount of documentation you will have over the course of an instructional year. Just what pieces are you or others going to use in making decisions and judgments about the student's progress? What is important? Is all of it important? These questions are significant when faced with a portfolio containing various bits and pieces of a student's learning process. Like a puzzle, you must put the pieces together to make an informed knowledgeable decision.

The limitations are not meant to prevent you from engaging in portfolio assessment. Rather, limitations are elements of the documentation portfolio that require you and your students to invest more effort in during the assessment process. It is certainly worth the effort and time. Meaningful evaluation leads to new ways of thinking and learning. The documentation portfolio offers insight into the learning process that your students are engaged in. Using documentation portfolios in your classroom adds "a depth to the picture of student development that is needed if educators are truly to understand individual student's strengths and needs" (Farnan & Kelly, 1991).

Evaluation Portfolio

A third type of portfolio found in classrooms is the evaluation portfolio. The evaluation portfolio is quite different in its purpose and in the collection of materials from the showcase and documentation portfolios. The purpose involved with an evaluation portfolio is to evaluate students on preselected tasks using predetermined criteria. Examples of evaluation portfolios come from state and district wide assessment practices and reform movements, including Vermont's Literacy Assessment Project and the reform efforts of California's Literacy Assessment System.

In serving the larger audience of district and state personnel, the evaluation portfolio strives to maintain consistency across classrooms and districts.

Within the parameters of an evaluation portfolio are specific tasks all students are required to complete. These predetermined tasks provide for the standardization of the portfolio. Specific selections enable evaluators to look systematically at students' work to make decisions regarding programs and curriculum. Often times included in these tasks are writing prompts, assigned topics, or problems with the context and criteria defined. Students are asked to complete the prompt using their own ideas and thoughts. Unlike the showcase and documentation portfolios, the evaluation portfolio's collection is dominated by tasks and activities selected by the teacher (Valencia & Calfee, 1991). There are attempts, however, to keep the items and artifacts as authentic as possible by selecting tasks and activities that meet the interests and needs of the students.

Student portfolios are then evaluated based on the preselected items. The rubrics and standards by which the students are judged are also predetermined, usually by outside agencies at the district or state level. In serving the larger audience of district and state personnel, the evaluation portfolio strives to maintain consistency across classrooms and districts.

Limitations of the Evaluation Portfolio

The evaluation portfolio is limited in authenticity and the student ownership process. Many of the artifacts included within the portfolio are not selected by the students. With others deciding on the items to be evaluated, the authenticity of the portfolio is at risk. Recall the definition of authenticity in assessment practices; it refers to an activity that is meaningful to students and is fundamentally instructive as opposed to evaluative (Smith, 1994). The evaluation portfolio is focused on judging student performance on specified tasks, thereby losing some of its authenticity for instructive purposes.

Additionally, the lack of student ownership in the portfolio is a limitation of this type of portfolio. Students have limited voice in the process and in the selection of materials to be evaluated on. There is little connection for the students between the instruction and teaching in the classroom and the predetermined tasks they are being asked to complete. Without the connection, ownership of the learning process is not evident. In the evaluation portfolio, students' voices about their own learning and the thinking processes they engage in are not heard.

These two limitations are especially significant if the evaluation portfolio is the only method of assessment being utilized. The evaluation portfolio is useful for district and state decisions regarding programs and curriculum, not for making decisions about individual students. Without the authenticity and student ownership of the process, it is quite difficult to construct and understand the many talents and abilities of the student. In most instances, an evaluation portfolio is separate from the entire assessment practice.

The items in the process portfolio are drawn from an integrated curriculum involving many tasks and concepts, including drafts, notes, and other pieces of evidence recording the learning process.

Process Portfolios

The fourth type of portfolio assessment practice recognized is the process portfolio (Valencia & Place, 1994). It is a portfolio of items and artifacts demonstrating work that is a part of a larger project. The purpose of the process portfolio is to document the learning process a student engages in through various projects throughout the instructional year. The learning process and self-reflection are highly valued in this portfolio. What makes the process portfolio different from the documentation portfolio, which has similar purposes, is the collection of materials.

Included within the process portfolio are samples of work that students engage in as they strive for the goals of the larger project. The items in the process portfolio are drawn from an integrated curriculum involving many tasks and concepts, including drafts, notes, and other pieces of evidence recording the learning process. What makes the process portfolio different from the documentation portfolio is not the purpose, but the type of items collected. In addition to the selected pieces of work, self-reflection is an important aspect of the process portfolio. Students reflect upon their own learning processes. Unlike the reflections in the showcase portfolio, the reflective comments in the process portfolio are focused on what was gained in the process; what steps were accomplished; what, if anything, would be changed in the future; and what the next steps will be in the process. Again, the examples on pages 19-20 can be used to begin the reflective process for your students.

The process portfolio is a method of assessing student growth in intervals. Rather than focusing on a student's progress over the entire course of a project, the process portfolio enables you to observe and evaluate student behavior and learning in smaller steps. The advantage in doing this is that you can align your curriculum and instructional decisions to best meet the needs of the student as the project progresses. For example, if you notice a student demonstrating difficulty in understanding certain concepts through the work being collected in the portfolio, you have the opportunity to alter your instruction to facilitate learning for the student. The process portfolio, therefore, promotes not only student learning but also opportunities for teachers to better integrate assessment and instructional practices.

The process portfolio, therefore, promotes not only student learning but also opportunities for teachers to better integrate assessment and instructional practices.

Limitations of the Process Portfolio

The process portfolio faces similar limitations as the other three types of portfolios. The difficulty in establishing standards and rubrics to evaluate the learning process is evident. Each student gains knowledge in unique and individual ways. The process will be different for each student. How do a teacher and the students determine a scale by which to make evaluative decisions about the learning process?

A second limitation of the process portfolio involves the exclusion of other points of view in the portfolio. In most cases, the student is responsible for selecting the items to be included. The teachers do not contribute their own perspectives and bits of information to the portfolio. A limited perspective emerges, and evaluators are asked to make instructional decisions based on the work and reflections provided by only the student. The process portfolio, while offering glimpses into the thinking and learning processes of students, does not offer the rich description that promotes informed, complete decisions.

Concluding Remarks

The four types of portfolios serve various needs and interests. Depending on the purposes established in your classroom, select one portfolio type that you believe to best serve the needs of you and your students. While there is no one portfolio that is comprehensive and without limitations, portfolio assessment practices are effective in evaluating your students' strengths and talents. Regardless of the type, portfolios bring assessment back into the classroom, involving your students and you in the process.

Issues to Consider

Three Important Issues to Think About

Portfolio assessment practices are complex and multifaceted. It is a process that has incredible potential to influence the teaching, learning, and assessment practices in classrooms throughout the country. Going beyond a collection of work in a folder to meaningful evaluation and decision making requires not only an understanding of the elements, the guidelines, and the various types of portfolios, but also an in-depth look at some of the issues now facing portfolio assessment implementation. These issues are not revolutionary, but they do impact the success of portfolios in your classroom. Integration is a significant concern to be considered. How do assessment practices influence instruction? Is it possible to integrate them? Student ownership of the assessment process is an issue that significantly impacts the success of the portfolio process. Will the student's voice be honored in the construction and evaluation of the portfolio? Additionally, management issues are critical to the effectiveness of the portfolios. How do teachers and students manage the new practice, including time, effort, and storage? These issues and questions are ones worth exploring.

It is a process that has incredible potential to influence the teaching, learning, and assessment practices in classrooms throughout the country.

Integration Between Assessment and Instruction

Portfolio assessment practices offer teachers opportunities to integrate instruction and assessment practices so that effective and meaningful instruction promotes effective and meaningful assessment and vice-versa. The alignment of the two practices is at the crux of successful teaching and learning. The integration of instructional and assessment practices is reflective of the purposes and goals established for the implementation of the portfolio. As students and teachers engage in the portfolio process, it is possible to determine the next instructional step by evaluating the selection of work the student has compiled for the portfolio. Does the student understand this concept? Has the student been engaged in the learning process? What gains has the student exhibited in acquiring knowledge? These questions and many others can be addressed as teachers and students reflect on the portfolios.

As a method of determining the next instructional step, portfolio assessment practices provide the teacher with valuable information and insight.

As a method of determining the next instructional step, portfolio assessment practices provide the teacher with valuable information and insight. Teachers can view the items collected in a portfolio and construct a picture of the student's learning process and abilities. Understanding what the student has accomplished in the activity and what knowledge was gained in the process enables the teacher to develop appropriate instructional activities to meet the student's needs.

Instruction and assessment should create an interrelated pathway, each influencing the other. As you evaluate your students' portfolios, not only will you judge their achievements but also make decisions regarding future activities and tasks. Portfolios provide you with information that is necessary as you plan your curriculum. Perhaps your students need more practice on a particular concept. You will be able to address this and plan accordingly based on the artifacts collected in the portfolio. Additionally, portfolios are instructive in assessing your own teaching strategies and techniques. Are your students making the academic gains you envisioned for them? Through portfolio assessment practices, you can develop and strengthen your own teaching strategies and curriculum activities.

Your students will come to see the circular pathway between instruction and assessment. The activities will become more meaningful and contextualized for the students. The alignment of instruction and assessment creates a student's awareness that what is taught is assessed, and the information gained from the assessment is meaningful and will be utilized. Interpreting the information in the portfolios will provide you with insight about your student's needs.

Student Ownership of the Process

This issue is probably the least talked about when implementing portfolio assessment practices in your classroom. What is meant by ownership? The portfolio enables students to have a voice in the assessment practice. The amount varies from an almost complete student decision in the showcase and process portfolios to an even distribution of decision making between the student and teacher in the documentation portfolio to limited student decision making in the evaluation portfolio.

Student ownership of the portfolio process is developed and encouraged as students become connected to the assessment practice. "Portfolios encourage students to retain ownership when students have personal reasons for developing portfolios, when they select the contents, and when they are invited to reflect on the very personal learning that their portfolios represent" (Paulson & Paulson, 1991, p. 296). All three of these factors have significant implications on the effectiveness and meaningfulness of the portfolio. Discussed throughout the chapters has been an underlying perspective that students must be involved in the decisions regarding the construction of their portfolios. These collaborative decisions will enable your students to come to the assessment practices with understanding and knowledge.

Providing your students with a voice in establishing the goals for the portfolios increases the motivation among them to participate in the process.

The discussions you and your students engage in regarding the purposes and reasons for the portfolio will promote motivation and interest in the students. When students are provided with choices in the learning paths taken, many of them have more desire to learn than when they must follow the paths prescribed by a teacher (Newkirk, 1991). Providing your students with a voice in establishing the goals for the portfolios increases the motivation among them to participate in the process. This increased motivation will encourage your students to develop a better understanding of the assessment and teaching practices in your classroom. They will have a sense of why the assessment practices occur and the importance attached to these practices. Discussing and establishing with your students the purposes, whether the portfolios will serve to document the learning process, to evaluate instructional practices, or to measure achievement across students, will provide your students with a clear understanding of the expectations you have for the portfolio practice.

The selection of the materials to be included in the portfolio is extremely important to the student participating in this assessment practice. Deciding what pieces of work will best represent her/his strengths according to the defined purposes is a decision that the student should have a voice in. The portfolio is a reflection of achievements and should be unique and individualized. Through the process of selecting the pieces, the construction of a portfolio enables a student to see that there is no single right way to portray the knowledge that has been gained.

There are instances, however, when your students may choose selections that you believe are not appropriate for the portfolios. What do you do? It is important to step back and ask yourself why the portfolio is being created, who the audience is for the portfolio, and why the student wants to include the specific piece. Creating meaningful portfolios requires that you, as the teacher, share the authority and decision making with your students. Allowing their decisions to be actualized is at the heart of the portfolio practice. Recognizing that portfolios are reflections of a student's achievements and beliefs, the choices made by the student should engage her/him in personal learning and knowledge building. This is a vital component of portfolio practices and cannot be ignored.

The portfolio is a reflection of achievements and should be unique and individualized.

The third factor encouraging student ownership is the self-reflection students participate in as they construct their portfolios. The reflective comments, both in oral discussion and in writing, enable students to develop clear understandings of the learning process in which they are engaged. The reflections provide students with opportunities to assess what was learned in the activity and what steps were taken to meet the established goals. Through reflection, students are able to determine the next step in the learning process. This understanding in turn promotes further engagement in the activities and learning process. Self-reflection, therefore, encourages student ownership of the portfolio assessment practice by affording opportunities to make explicit their insights into their own course of learning.

Student ownership of the portfolio assessment practice "place[s] students in the position of learning to assess themselves, share who they are with others, and set their own learning goals" (Tierney, 1994, p. 232). Ownership of learning and assessment processes empowers students and teachers in a way they have never experienced before. As you encourage your students to participate and own the assessment practices, complete and meaningful pictures of their strengths and abilities are brought into focus. Their voices are heard, and through these voices, the complex and multifaceted dimensions of the student as a learner emerge.

Management of the Portfolio Practice

Unlike integration and student ownership, management of the portfolio practice is most frequently questioned by teachers. How is it possible to collect and organize all the pieces of work for each student? How does one have the time to evaluate the work and make appropriate judgments based on the collected work? What kind of support and training is available to help understand the complexities of authentic assessment practices? These questions are but a few that many teachers are asking. They are not easy to answer. Portfolios require time, effort, and many revisions along the way.

Alternative assessment practices, and especially portfolios, are time intensive. You will need time to establish the purposes for the portfolios and develop the rubrics by which student portfolios will be evaluated. Teachers engaging their students in the decision making process will have to utilize instructional time to discuss the various facets of the portfolio process. Once these are established, time is needed to gather and interpret the various pieces of information provided by the student. The gathered information is often from a variety of contexts. The diversity of materials in the portfolio requires that time is spent in an effort to make connections between the pieces to effectively summarize your student's performance and abilities. It is more complex and involved to assess a student's understandings through the diverse and extensive samples of work than it is to interpret a single score achieved through traditional assessment practices. In addition, you will want to engage your students in self-reflection and discussions about their portfolios. Portfolios, therefore, are time consuming, no doubt about it. It is a practice, however, that is worth the time because you will develop a more complete picture of the students, and in turn meet the needs of the students more effectively.

You will need time to establish the purposes for the portfolios and develop the rubrics by which student portfolios will be evaluated.

Another management issue comes in storing the many artifacts and items. Most teachers implementing portfolio assessment practices in their classrooms have devised a system they can handle and work with. The system varies from teacher to teacher, reflecting individual personalities and styles. Again, it is also dependent on the purposes for the portfolios. Teachers use boxes, folders, containers, cabinets, etc. You will have to experiment and create your own system. A factor you will want to consider is student access. Will the students and other interested parties have access to the portfolios at any time? Specified times? The access will impact the storing of the portfolios, whether students keep them in desks to be handled at any time or they are placed somewhere in the classroom with limited access.

Training and support from colleagues are two other factors influencing management of portfolios. It is important that teachers engaging in portfolio assessment practices have some training in the process. There is much to consider when embarking on this new practice, including establishing rubrics and criteria, understanding the learning and teaching perspectives underlying the portfolio practice, and addressing viewpoints on student ownership and reflection. Many teachers have not had to face these issues and consequently have limited experience. Teachers need opportunities to learn how to interpret the information in the portfolios and develop narratives on those interpretations.

Embarking on portfolio assessment practice is difficult. It is important that teachers have the opportunity to share their experiences with colleagues. The feedback and collaboration provided by other teachers support and encourage continued reflection about the portfolio process and whether the assessment needs are being met. Through the support and collaboration teachers gain confidence and understanding as they effectively utilize portfolios in their classrooms.

The feedback and collaboration provided by other teachers support and encourage continued reflection about the portfolio process and whether the assessment needs are being met.

Concluding Remarks

Portfolios offer many teachers and students new perspectives and insights into the teaching and learning process. Issues to be considered as you develop portfolio assessment practices include integration of instruction and assessment, student ownership of the process, and management. These issues are important to the success of portfolios in your classroom because they impact decisions made about students and their progress. Integrating instruction and assessment makes sense. Teachers should use the information provided in their students' portfolios to make informed instructional decisions. Student ownership is not only an important issue of portfolios but is tied to the authenticity of assessment and learning. Student ownership instills responsibility for the learning process and development in the individual student. And management is an issue that if not faced will cause portfolios to collapse. Teachers must take into consideration the time and effort portfolios require. All three of these issues ask teachers and students to be actively involved in the portfolio assessment practice. This involvement will render authentic, substantive, meaningful evaluations and judgments of students and the learning processes.

Constructing Professional Development Portfolios

Why Construct Teacher Portfolios?

Just as teachers are beginning to ask their students to construct portfolios for evaluation purposes, teachers are also beginning to see the value in constructing their own portfolios. Professional development portfolios enable teachers to reflect on and evaluate their own teaching practices, thus recognizing the diversity and complexity of the profession. Through the professional development portfolio, you will come to view yourself and your practices differently. "Portfolios provide one path to a possible reframing of the educational enterprise" (Graham, 1993, p. 24). Professional development portfolios offer opportunities for teachers to engage in dialogue with other participants in the education system. The dialogue promotes new directions and expanded views of teaching and learning.

Professional development portfolios offer opportunities for teachers to engage in dialogue with other participants in the education system.

Purposes and Artifacts

Professional development portfolios are as unique and individualized as student portfolios. Depending on the purposes established for the portfolio, the materials collected will vary among teachers. One use of the portfolio is to evaluate a teacher's performance.

Administrators are now beginning to assess teachers through their portfolios. When portfolios are used for evaluative purposes, you will want to include artifacts that reflect your abilities and strengths as a teacher. This is similar to a showcase portfolio. The best work is in the professional portfolio: lessons that went well, students' work that demonstrates a learning process, professional growth activities that are effective and meaningful in the classroom, etc. Another use of the portfolio involves observing patterns and behaviors of a teacher. If you are interested in recording actions and strategies in your teaching practice, a documentation type portfolio will better serve the purpose. As in a student portfolio, a documentation type of professional development portfolio includes many sources of materials from a variety of perspectives. Teachers are able to engage in self-reflection as they come to understand their teaching practices.

When portfolios are used for evaluative purposes, you will want to include artifacts that reflect your abilities and strengths as a teacher.

Additionally, the evaluation and process types of portfolios are also possible as professional development portfolios. For the evaluation type, an administrator for the district and/or state would establish the criteria for teacher performance. An evaluator may want to assess how you construct a thematic unit and will be looking for specified criteria to be met. A process portfolio for professional development may take on the characteristics of folders for mini-units. As you develop an integrated, thematic unit, you may store and collect items in a process portfolio. The process portfolio enables a teacher to revisit the initial goals and objectives and to stay focused on them.

For teachers engaging in professional development portfolios, the showcase and documentation types are the most common. Teachers are comfortable displaying their best and reflecting on how successful particular lessons and activities were. Many teachers are not particularly comfortable having their teaching practice evaluated on predetermined standards as in the evaluation portfolio. Nor is the process portfolio as clearly defined as some would like it to be. However, no matter what type of portfolio is being implemented, the collected materials and samples in the professional development portfolio provide you and others in the educational process with tools to critically examine the instructional practices in the classroom.

The selection of materials collected for a teacher portfolio will represent the teacher's own philosophy of teaching and education and the purposes being served. Examples of items in a professional development portfolio might include sample lesson plans, assignments, tests, students' work sample,; written feedback to students or from students, reflective statement,; correspondence with parents, colleagues, and administration, and evidence of professional growth activities such as workshops, in-service workshops, classes, etc. (Graham, 1993). The collected items should reflect the roles and activities teachers engage in with students and others in the educational process.

Growth Through Professional Portfolios

Professional development portfolios create a personal record of the beliefs and values held by the individual teacher. This record becomes explicit when you discuss your portfolio. Discussions center around the collected materials, the reasons for including them into the portfolio, and the information gained in the process. Professional development portfolios promote critical reflection on the activities you engage in while teaching. Questions to consider as you participate in self-reflection include:

Self-reflection opens the door to new possibilities and paradigms of teaching and thinking.

- Are those activities found in your portfolio proven to be worthwhile and effective in your practice?
- Are your students learning in the manner you anticipated?
- What types of instructional decisions are you making over the course of the year as documented in the portfolio?
- What are the defining characteristics of the successful lessons you taught?
- What information did you gain in reviewing the correspondence between you and others?
- How does the portfolio reflect you as a teacher?

The selected materials and items in your professional development portfolio will assist you in answering these questions and others related to your teaching and instructional practices. Self-reflection opens the door to new possibilities and paradigms of teaching and thinking. Through reflection you are able to revisit choices and decisions. By examining your actions and perspectives, you can thoughtfully consider and expand upon them, leading to multiple paths of teaching and learning. Your expanded views of teaching and learning will in turn offer new possibilities for your students. The recurring nature of teaching and learning encourages reflection. The reflections you have about your practices will provide opportunities for you to "decide ways of proceeding, to choose among alternative pathways, or to gain new understandings about yourself, the context of the situation, and your unquestioned assumptions about practice" (Graham, 1993, p. 34).

In addition to self-reflection, professional development portfolios offer teachers opportunities to share with their peers and others in the educational process. Teaching is an isolating profession. Rarely are there opportunities to engage in and contribute to an ongoing professional dialogue, discussing new paradigms in teaching and learning. Professional development portfolios provide teachers with a situated frame of reference. Teachers can come together and with their portfolios have a shared context in which to begin the conversations. Engaging in professional dialogues creates a positive atmosphere where teachers can grow, develop, and collaborate. As you open your portfolio to others the conversations will offer new perceptions and perspectives. As a professional, you will take from the conversations and dialogue valuable insights and information. Perhaps you will learn new techniques from your colleagues or will provide your colleagues with insights of your own. Professional collaborations can also occur as you discover others' interests and projects. Professional development portfolios open the door to professional dialogues and collaborations.

Professional dialogues initiated by professional development portfolios provide teachers with starting points for those conversations which lead to renewed perspectives on thinking and learning.

Imagine, if you will, an opportunity to engage in a professional conversation with a colleague. The conversation is not by chance or random, but rather one that is purposefully designed to discover the talents and strengths you each offer to the profession. You both bring to the conversation portfolios that you have been developing throughout the instructional year. What are you going to share with your colleague? What do you want to discover about her/him? What are your colleague's strengths? What can you learn from this peer? What information can you offer her/him? Discussing with your colleague how your portfolio reflects you as a teacher will demand clarity in your thinking about teaching and learning. As you engage in professional dialogue, you both will construct a shared frame of reference on which to base future actions. The new actions will have as their history the voices from your conversation. Your newly constructed insights about teaching and learning will extend into other conversations. Each conversation develops and builds, restructuring the ideas and perceptions held about the practice of teaching. Professional dialogues initiated by professional development portfolios provide teachers with starting points for those conversations which lead to renewed perspectives on thinking and learning.

Other aspects of professional development portfolios contributing to the growth and development of a teacher's practice involve accountability and ownership. A professional portfolio records activities and actions by an individual teacher in the course of a specified time period. As you participate in discussions about the artifacts in your portfolio, you will justify the existence of those items. Being able to clearly articulate the purposes and rationale you have for the collected items promotes accountability and ownership of the process. You are accountable for understanding and justifying your teaching practices in the classroom. There may be times when you have difficulty articulating and explaining items in the portfolio. Discussing your teaching practices is a skill that must be developed. The process of self-reflection will assist in critically assessing the goals and intentions you had for an activity. Were my teaching strategies appropriate for the students in my classroom? Was the activity suited to their needs? As you engage in self-reflective techniques and skills when discussing your professional portfolio, you will gain knowledge and insight into your own teaching practices and beliefs, further promoting accountability for your actions.

Ownership of the teaching process becomes more explicit as a teacher constructs a professional development portfolio. The freedom to build a portfolio created solely through your actions and decisions is inspiring. The decisions involved in constructing a professional portfolio and in sharing the contents of the portfolio with others is empowering. A professional portfolio enables you to contribute your thoughts and ideas about teaching and learning to the educational community. Portfolios are public. They are created so that you and others can reflect on the actions taken in a classroom. The professional development portfolio promotes ownership and empowerment of the teaching and learning process by making explicit your ideas and beliefs. As you engage in the process of developing a portfolio, opportunities to make decisions regarding your students' instructional program and your interactions with them increase. You are empowered to reflect on and assess your teaching strategies, all of which leads to having ownership of the teaching process and making decisions as to the paths to be taken.

Participating in constructing a professional development portfolio enables teachers to view the teaching process as the complex, multifaceted process that it is.

Concluding Remarks

Participating in constructing a professional development portfolio enables teachers to view the teaching process as the complex, multifaceted process that it is. The portfolio you create will provide opportunities to reflect upon your own practice and strategies, engage in professional dialogue with peers and colleagues, collaborate on various projects and ideas, and expand your perceptions of accountability and ownership. The professional development portfolio "is the personal record of the individual teacher wherein the teacher defines his/her situation, interprets what is seen to be important and documents the practices that were applied" (Graham, 1993, p. 34). As you engage in developing a professional portfolio to gain understanding and insight into your teaching practices, you will experience similar frustrations and accomplishments as your students. Creating portfolios that accurately reflect you and your beliefs is not an easy process, nor is it easy for your students. There will be many shifts in the selection of items to be included, and you may shift perspectives as you articulate your reflections. What are you going to choose, and what information is to be gained from the process? How can you critically assess your teaching? What changes in your own thinking patterns will impact the gathering of items for the portfolio? How do you present your portfolio to your colleagues, the administration, parents? Answering these questions and others encourages you to grow and develop as a professional. The change in how you perceive yourself and your actions as a teacher offers new perspectives of both yourself and the teaching process. New meanings are established within the profession, expanding perceptions of teaching and learning.

Portfolios Across the Curriculum

Portfolios Offer New Perspectives

Portfolio assessment practices have in recent years been most closely associated with evaluating students' writing processes. Teachers have students collect various samples of writing to demonstrate their growth and development as writers. Many teachers and students are comfortable with this evaluation method for writing because writing is viewed as a developmental process, and it is possible to document the growth without too much additional thought or work. Content areas such as reading, science, math, and social studies have not found their way into the portfolio arena as readily. The students' performances in these subjects, however, can be effectively and meaningfully evaluated through portfolios. Portfolio assessment practices go beyond evaluating writing and offer students and teachers new ways of viewing the learning process in many different content areas.

Portfolio assessment practices go beyond evaluating writing and offer students and teachers new ways of viewing the learning process in many different content areas.

Constructing portfolios across the curriculum provides opportunities to experience the developmental nature of learning in all subjects. Students and teachers selecting best work and pieces demonstrating understanding of a particular concept encourage a renewed interest in learning as a process rather than a product. Portfolio assessment practices in all curricular subjects focuses the learning process on the steps taken to achieve a desired goal. For example, a student develops a math portfolio. Included in the portfolio are samples of work depicting a student's attempts to solve an open ended math problem. The initial actions that failed to reach the desired solution are represented in the samples. The teacher and student can now view the learning process that this student engaged in and make a meaningful decision as to the next step to take in the instructional process.

While recognizing that many teachers are now implementing an integrated curriculum, some may desire to have specified subject portfolios. As students develop portfolios in the specified subjects, the entire process becomes more manageable. The portfolio represents a subject and the knowledge gained in that subject, rather than a storehouse of work. Students and teachers can more effectively evaluate the learning that has occurred if there is a common base. In this case, the base is the subject, such as reading, math, science, or social studies. The purposes for the portfolios, the types of portfolios, and the evaluation standards do not change in focus or intent. The differences in the content area portfolios are only in the materials collected.

The meanings and interpretations students and teachers create from the portfolios are based on complex negotiations among the student, the teacher, peers, and the situation itself.

Literacy Portfolios

Portfolios of work documenting progress in reading and writing are the most common in many classrooms. In recent years the focus in reading and writing has shifted from a collection of discrete, isolated skills to viewing reading and writing as an integrated process within a meaningful context. Reading and writing support each other. The interconnectedness and integration of reading and writing in the curriculum have enabled students to construct portfolios that reflect the shared meanings that occur as students learn to read and write. The meanings and interpretations students and teachers create from the portfolios are based on complex negotiations among the student, the teacher, peers, and the situation itself. These newly established negotiations sustain the authenticity and effectiveness of portfolios as an assessment practice. Literacy portfolios support the learning perspective that literacy develops as a process of emerging expertise. Rather than a set of isolated skills to be evaluated on, there is a central goal to be built upon which recurs from one situation to the next (Pearson, 1994). Through a portfolio, emerging understandings are visible to both the creator and the evaluator.

Deciding on the samples of work to include in a literacy portfolio is an individual process, both for the student and the situation. Recalling that the decisions should be as collaborative as possible, you and your student should discuss the items and the reasons for including them in the portfolio based on the purposes and intentions previously established. Examples of such items that may be found in a literacy portfolio are reading logs, journal entries, interest surveys, responses to literature, various pieces of writing depicting the different stages in the writing process, a variety of genre pieces, observational and anecdotal notes, student and teacher reflections, and other samples that demonstrate to the evaluator the accomplishments and achievements of the student on reading and writing activities. To provide some initial structure to the selection process and then to the evaluation, a suggestion is to have a couple of pieces of work in the portfolio that all of your students complete. This will help to establish a framework for understanding the nature of literacy and the activities involved in your classroom.

Science Portfolios

The development and use of portfolios in the content area of science can be an important step in effectively assessing the knowledge and insights students gain in science. Scientific knowledge stretches beyond defining isolated terms and facts and incorporates an array of thinking skills and processes. The evaluation of the knowledge should do the same. Science portfolios enable students to demonstrate they can construct knowledge that represents the concepts and processes of science and to capture the excitement that is inherent in science activities and experiments (Collins, 1992). Through their participation in constructing science portfolios, teachers and students experience the complexities of science, ranging from explaining and predicting natural events in science to asking questions and to working in a group on an experiment.

Scientific knowledge stretches beyond defining isolated terms and facts and incorporates an array of thinking skills and processes.

The items in a science portfolio have the potential to encompass many components of the science curriculum. Important to remember are the goals and purposes for the activities and the portfolios. What are the students expected to gain from the science activities? What type of portfolio is going to be constructed, such as showcase, documentation, evaluation, or process? Depending on the type of portfolio, tasks such as observations, predictions, recordings, understandings of basic scientific concepts, data collections, definitions, discussions, experiments, classifications, comparisons, inferences, and reflections may be included in the portfolio. Also included may be the notes you take while observing your students as they engage in various science tasks. What did you notice? What steps did the student take to reach a goal? While the items in a science portfolio are generally written documents, they do not need to be limited to that. Drawings, models, photographs, graphs, and charts should also be included if appropriate to the goals and needs. Science portfolios provide opportunities to document the various thinking skills and abilities in a well developed science curriculum.

Again, self-reflection is a critical component of portfolios, including science portfolios. The reflections can incorporate many aspects of science. Asking students to discuss their experiences when working on an experiment in a group setting, to reflect on the initial predictions made compared to the outcomes received, to reflect on the steps taken to achieve a desired outcome, and to discuss relationships and connections to other scientific concepts requires effort and time. Encourage reflective thinking from your students about the progress they are achieving in science. Self-reflection on science activities will provide your students with the tools to make meaningful and purposeful connections between science and other activities in their lives, thereby increasing the relevance and authenticity of the science curriculum.

Science portfolios provide opportunities to document the various thinking skills and abilities in a well developed science curriculum.

To assist in the management of science portfolios, you might want to include a form that itemizes and lists the various pieces of work within the portfolio. Utilizing a form similar to the checklists discussed earlier will enable you to quickly and easily determine what items are located in the portfolio and what items may be missing. The form on the following page is an example that may be used as science portfolios are constructed in your classroom. As a reminder, the form is science specific but can be adapted for any content area portfolio.

What is in Here?

Name ______________________________ Date _________________________

The science portfolio before you contains the following items for display:

Recorded observations on ____

____

Predictions about ____

____

Comparisons between ____

____

Projects on ____

____

Self-reflections on ____

____

Teacher notes and observations ____________________________________

____

Scoring rubrics for ____

____

Other interesting items ____

____

Math Portfolios

Similar to science portfolios, constructing portfolios for the content area of math is a meaningful and effective method for assessing students' thinking and learning processes involving mathematical concepts. The trend in recent years has been on a problem solving curriculum with an emphasis on understanding that most authentic problems can not be solved quickly and often have many more than one answer. Students are assessed on such aspects as using mathematics to make sense of complex situations, ability to use mathematical processes such as computation in the context of many kinds of problems rather than in isolation, defining and formulating problems, and explaining a mathematical concept either orally or in writing (California Mathematics Council, 1991). Constructing math portfolios enables students to demonstrate their mathematical thinking processes in a variety of ways.

Math portfolios also have within their boundaries many different types of work and samples.

Math portfolios have many advantages in assessing the strengths and talents of your students. The items in the portfolios often provide evidence of performance and understanding that go beyond factual knowledge. Students are able to perform tasks and activities through a variety of learning styles and modalities, thereby eliminating the dependence on end of unit and timed tests. A math portfolio also encourages integration with other content areas, particularly writing. Students include written accounts of the math problems and solutions. These mathematical writings enhance the learning process by providing opportunities to formulate, organize, internalize, and evaluate mathematical concepts. Math portfolios encourage students and teachers to perceive mathematical concepts from a new perspective.

Math portfolios also have within their boundaries many different types of work and samples. Students can include such items as written descriptions of different investigations and problems, pictures, graphs and charts, responses to open-ended questions, group reports and solutions, descriptions and diagrams of problem solving processes, activities and tasks utilizing a variety of mathematical tools and models such as manipulatives, calculators, and computers, and group projects. Including these types of samples in the portfolio will allow students to demonstrate their strategies and techniques in solving open- ended problems, requiring them to think and reason and not just calculate answers.

The reflective pieces students write to include in their math portfolios help them assess their growth and achievements in understanding mathematical concepts. The reflections provide students with opportunities to review their own performance, explain the reasons for choosing the processes they used, and identify the next step to be taken (California Mathematics Council, 1991). The reflection process helps students build confidence when they gauge their own performance and observe their growth and development in math. Building math confidence is critical to the success students achieve in learning mathematical concepts. Self-reflections in math portfolios communicate to the student and the teacher the thinking patterns and processes that went into solving the math problems.

Math portfolios provide opportunities to engage students and teachers in the entire process of learning. Students are able to demonstrate their mathematical understandings in a variety of ways for a variety of tasks. Teachers can evaluate a student's knowledge by assessing the whole of the portfolio rather than individual pieces of work. With the whole of the math portfolio in mind, you can examine work samples to see what your student knows about particular mathematical concepts, and note how the student's understanding has developed over time along with how her/his thinking has been clarified (Ferguson, 1992). You are also able to determine whether the student missed key concepts or did not understand, and therefore, will require additional help. A mathematics portfolio will enable the teacher or other evaluator to try and "get a picture of the student's own thinking rather than whether the student can provide the 'correct' answer that the adult has in mind" (California Mathematics Council, 1991, p.23). Is the student merely giving memorized responses, or has the student interacted with the ideas and incorporated them into her/his own thinking and knowledge structures? Math portfolios provide the insights necessary to effectively and meaningfully evaluate student performance.

Teachers can evaluate a student's knowledge by assessing the whole of the portfolio rather than individual pieces of work.

Social Studies Portfolios

Also appearing on the circuit of portfolio trends are portfolios in social studies. As with the other content areas, social studies instruction and curriculum have a new focus and perspective. Students are no longer memorizing decontextualized, isolated facts to be reproduced on multiple choice exams. Rather the focus has changed to integrating social studies concepts with other content areas in an authentic context. Often a theme is associated with such social studies concepts as "Family and Communities," "State History," or "American Life Before 1776." Students gather information from a variety of sources outside the textbook such as literature and primary sources such as letters, speeches, and diaries to make the social studies curriculum interactive and dynamic (Ryan, 1994). With the information available from a variety of sources, the portfolio assessment practice is an appropriate method to assess the student's knowledge and concept development. Social studies portfolios encourage students to demonstrate their abilities and strengths in utilizing many sources of information to make informed decisions over a period of time.

Included within a social studies portfolio are many different types of items. The pieces of work selected for the portfolio will reflect the curriculum strands being developed in a grade level. The strands range from history and geography to culture and ethnic belief systems. The samples are usually integrated activities and tasks involving writing, reading, math, and science. Students may want to include such items as journals, responses to literature and historical figures and events, predictive tasks and events, map and globe activities, pictures and drawings depicting different events and scenes, self-reflections on selected work, surveys and interest forms, and research projects. Group projects may also be included if students are working in cooperative groups to complete a task. Photographs in the portfolio enable all participants to have a representation of the project. These items and others are useful in constructing a social studies portfolio.

The pieces of work selected for the portfolio will reflect the curriculum strands being developed in a grade level.

Cooperative group activities are frequently used in a social studies curriculum. The group activities develop students' abilities to work with each other, accept group decisions, and develop interpersonal skills. Within the group there are a variety of roles and responsibilities students are to assume, from supplier (the student getting supplies and materials) to the timekeeper (the student who keeps the group on task) to the reporter (the student who reports information to the class). Additional responsibilities and roles can be added to the group depending on the need. After a cooperative group has worked on a task, what information can be added to the students' individual social studies portfolios to reflect their participation in the task? Students can each complete forms reflecting on the results of their products and on the processes of working with others. Samples of such reflection forms are on the next two pages.

How Did We Do?

Assignment: Date:

Group Members

As a group, decide which face you should circle for the first two statements. Then, complete the remaining sentences.

1. We finished our job on time and did a good job.
2. We encouraged each other and cooperated with each other.
3. We did best at ____________________
4. Next time we could improve at ____________________

Reprinted from TCM Workshop Notebook "Portfolios and Other Alternative Assessments", *Teacher Created Materials, 1993*

Student Checklist
Cooperative Learning Groups

Name ____________________ Activity: ____________________

Check off the following if you were a responsible group member.

_______ Followed directions carefully and quietly.

_______ Used a quiet voice when speaking.

_______ Knew my job in the group and did it.

_______ Stayed on task.

_______ Asked questions politely.

_______ Took turns politely.

_______ Encouraged others (no put-downs).

_______ Was a good example for others.

_______ Contributed my best ideas and behavior to the group.

_______ Stayed with the group until the activity was complete.

Reprinted from TCM Workshop Notebook "Portfolios and Other Alternative Assessments", *Teacher Created Materials, 1993*

Including information about how students perceive their abilities in working cooperatively in groups will provide you with invaluable insights as to the actions and behaviors of your students. The forms enable your students to look at not only how successful they were in meeting the objectives of the task but also how well they worked together (Jasmine, 1994).

Social studies portfolios are an effective method for assessing the learning processes of your students. The portfolios enable both the student and you to document and record growth and development in social studies concepts over time. The authenticity of participating in activities and tasks that are integrated with other content areas and utilizing many sources of information are meaningful ways to gain knowledge and insights in the content area of social studies. Evaluation of these tasks and activities is best accomplished through portfolio assessment practices.

Social studies portfolios are an effective method for assessing the learning processes of your students.

Concluding Remarks

Portfolios constructed for the different content areas of literacy, science, math, and social studies are effective and meaningful in evaluating student growth and progress in those areas. By organizing the information gathered by students and you into content areas, it is possible to document the achievements and strengths of students in the specific subject.

The first content portfolio highlighted was the literacy portfolio. Literacy portfolios include artifacts and samples of student work in reading and writing. The interrelationship of these two areas supports the use of portfolios as an effective method of assessment.

Science and math portfolios offer students and teachers opportunities to appreciate and understand the complexities of learning science and math processes. Students can document knowledge and understanding of concepts such as observations, classification, inferences, formulations, and organization. The portfolios encourage students to reflect on their development in science and math through a variety of perspectives.

The fourth content area portfolio is the social studies portfolio. Students engage in creating social studies portfolios to demonstrate knowledge gathered through a variety of sources for a particular unit of study. The social studies portfolio also provides opportunities for cooperative groups to acknowledge and document their processes as they develop group skills.

Portfolio assessment practices across the curriculum enable the new perspectives in teaching and learning to be realized. In all content areas, the focus on learning has moved from an isolated skill approach to an integrated, contextualized approach. Portfolios offer opportunities for teachers and students to evaluate not only the products but also the learning processes involved.

Last Thoughts, Future Directions

Synthesis of Ideas

Portfolio assessment practices are infusing themselves into many classrooms across the country. Teachers are changing their teaching practices and beliefs based on new perspectives of and insights about the learning process. The new perspectives advocate learning as a process that is best achieved in an integrated, authentic context. Thinking about learning as a process is requiring new approaches to activities and tasks. Students are engaged in open-ended discovery tasks with many solutions and answers. Students are being asked to think about and consider a variety of options, as opposed to a single right answer. There are more cooperative group activities occurring in classrooms, asking students to produce results in a group format. These changes in instructional practices are impacting the assessment practices teachers and students engage in. It is no longer possible to adequately and effectively assess a student's performance based on a single exam. Rather, teachers and students are valuing the multidimensional perspective alternative assessment practices offer, especially portfolios.

It is no longer possible to adequately and effectively assess a student's performance based on a single exam.

Portfolios are perhaps the alternative assessment method that has received the most attention in classrooms and districts throughout the nation. At first glance, portfolios appear to be simple and relatively easy to implement. You have your students collect work in a folder and you look through the materials at a later date. This scenario is not uncommon. Many teachers and other educators in district and state offices operate under that assumption. Hopefully, you have gained a new perspective in the complexities of portfolio assessment practices.

Portfolios are dynamic, interactive, and multidimensional. They provide students and teachers with many opportunities to assess students' performances on a variety of levels. As you begin to develop portfolio assessment practices in your classroom, it is important to address the aspects and elements of portfolios that make the practice an effective assessment of students' learning processes. Understanding different types of portfolios and the issues that surround them are also critical to achieving the assessment results you intend. Portfolios are more than folders. They are evidence of students' constructions of knowledge structures that will carry them onto future paths of learning.

Understanding different types of portfolios and the issues that surround them are also critical to achieving the assessment results you intend.

Thoughts to pursue as you establish portfolio assessment practices in your classroom include the elements and guidelines of meaningful assessments. The five elements of portfolios involve (1) collaboration between you and your students regarding decisions about the purposes and intentions of the portfolios and the contents to be included, (2) incorporating an expanded view of learning recognizing diversity and complexity in the learning process, (3) understanding that learning is a process and that any student's learning unfolds over time and in many different contexts, (4) exploring and valuing the multiple perspectives of learning and development, and (5) incorporating reflection and self-assessment into the process. Collaboration and reflection are critical to the success of portfolio assessment practices. Both elements ask teachers and students to engage in the process of assessment, thereby empowering their perspectives and voices. Collaboration offers opportunities for shared understandings, and reflection provides explicitness in determining the significance of the activity and the process. The five elements are necessary considerations as your students construct portfolios to be used for assessment purposes. They provide the underlying base for meaningful portfolios.

The next level to contemplate in effective portfolio assessment practices are the guidelines of evaluation. What is taken into consideration as you and other evaluators view your students' portfolios? The guidelines of evaluation involve establishing standards and rubrics, defining the audience which will be assessing the portfolios, and determining the purposes to be served through the construction of the portfolios. These guidelines should be established prior to the construction of portfolios. It is important that students participate in creating the rubrics and standards by which they will be judged. The standards and rubrics should reflect and refer to what is valued by those involved in the process. Establishing rubrics requires clarity in what the expectations are for students' performances.

The audience can impact significantly the outcomes of the portfolio. The different audiences, such as teacher, parents, peers, district and state personnel come to the portfolio with their own frames of reference and individual value systems. Information they gain from the portfolio will be reflective of their own thinking and beliefs.

Portfolios serve many purposes. Clearly articulating the identified purposes and intentions has significant impact on the success of the portfolios as an assessment practice. The purpose is defined by those involved. "A portfolio is whatever the community using the portfolio wants it to be" (Collins, 1992, p. 452). The purpose often includes documenting student growth over time, encouraging student ownership and decision making, reflecting and influencing curriculum decisions, representing the processes and products involved. The multifaceted nature of the purposes in portfolios requires that purposes be established prior to the collection of materials and the evaluation of those materials.

Clearly articulating the identified purposes and intentions has significant impact on the success of the portfolios as an assessment practice.

Further last thoughts include understanding the different types of portfolios and their benefits and limitations. All portfolios have benefits and limitations. It is important to think about the purposes you have in mind for your students and their portfolios and then match a portfolio type to those purposes. The types of portfolios, again, are showcase, documentation, evaluation, and process. Generally, you will find the showcase and documentation implemented in classrooms. While limitations can put portfolio assessment practices in a negative light, you should take a moment to truly assess what is meant by a limitation. For the most part, the limitations were identified to provide you with aspects to consider before engaging in developing portfolios in your classroom, not to discourage their use.

Additional issues to ponder as you engage in portfolio assessment practices involve integration between assessment and curriculum, management of the process, and ownership of the process and products. The interrelated nature of instruction and assessment should be evident in portfolios. The information gained in evaluating student growth and performance should influence the next steps to be taken in instruction. As instruction and assessment practices align themselves with each other, the activities and tasks students engage in should be more meaningful and contextualized. Each practice influences the other, creating a circular pathway between instruction and assessment.

Managing portfolio assessment practices is more involved and complex than traditional assessment practices. Creating systems to handle the amount of artifacts collected and scheduling additional time are important to assure the success of portfolios. Portfolio assessment practices require more effort and thought but result in creating complete pictures of your students' strengths and talents in many areas. You are able to evaluate the whole of your student rather than isolated pieces that may not give an accurate picture of the student's performance.

You are able to evaluate the whole of your student rather than isolated pieces that may not give an accurate picture of the student's performance.

Other issues critical to the successful construction of portfolios are ownership and empowerment. Through portfolios, the voices of students in your classroom and your own voice can be heard as decisions are made regarding the purposes for the portfolios, the materials to be collected, and the ways in which those items will be evaluated. Decisions affecting instructional practices can also utilize the information in portfolios. Portfolios offer opportunities for students and teachers to see there is no single correct way to put together a portfolio but that the choices are theirs and the possibilities have been expanded. Decision making is an important aspect of portfolios. Portfolios provide ownership and empowerment in the teaching and learning processes.

All of these aspects of portfolios; elements, guidelines, and issues are reflected in meaningful and effective uses of portfolios in classrooms. They are numerous and can be overwhelming as you think about implementing portfolio assessment practices with your students. They do, however, provide the difference between folders and authentic, alternative assessment practices.

Making the leap between these options is not an easy process. Trying to incorporate all of the addressed aspects at once will leave you frustrated with the entire process. Start small. Portfolio assessment practices are flexible. Begin where you are most comfortable. As you gain knowledge and expertise you can expand the portfolio assessment practice to other areas of the curriculum. Before you realize it, you will be engaged in implementing a meaningful assessment practice.

As a place to start, you might be interested in constructing your own portfolio. The professional development portfolio can provide you with opportunities to experiment with various activities such as reflection. Recognizing the difficulties you experience will enable you to have a better perspective of the process you are asking your students to undertake. Also, the content area portfolios are ways to make the portfolio assessment process more manageable. Limiting the items to be collected to one content area will give you a base to start with. These two suggestions as places to start with portfolio assessment practices are just that, suggestions. Start with the process wherever you want and go from there. Important to the portfolio process is that you and your students are active, contributing members of the assessment practice. The interactive nature of a portfolio encourages students and teachers to reflect on what is occurring in the classroom and in the thinking processes of the members of the classroom.

Portfolio assessment practices are no longer only for artists and craftsmen. Students and teachers are engaging in the process of constructing portfolios to better understand the complexities of learning and teaching. As a multifaceted method of assessing the growth and development of learning, portfolios offer many possibilities to students and teachers. It is possible to glimpse the thought process of students as they pave their road of achievements.

References

Au, K. & Jordan, C. (1982). Teaching reading to Hawaiian children: Finding a culturally appropriate solution. In H.T. Trueba, G.P. Guthrie, & K.H. Au (Eds.), Culture in the bilingual classroom: Studies in classroom ethnography (pp. 153-177). Rowley, MA: Newbury House.

Biggam, S. (1994). Seeing the big picture: Using a multilevel, multidimensional rubric to enhance primary-level portfolio assessment. Unpublished manuscript.

California Mathematics Council (1991). Assessment alternatives in mathematics. Sacramento, CA: California State Department of Education.

Chamot, A. (1980, November). Recent research on second-language reading. NCBA Forum (pp. 3-4).

Collins, A. (1992). Portfolios for science education: Issues in purpose, structure, and authenticity. Science Education, 76, 451-463.

Cooper, W. (1994). Staff development for portfolios and portfolio assessment. Portfolio News, 5, (2), 2-4.

Farnan, N. & Kelly, P. (1991). Keeping track: Creating assessment portfolios in reading and writing. Reading, Writing, and Learning Disabilities, 7, 255-269.

Farr, R. & Beck, M. (1991). Formal methods of evaluation. In J. Flood, J. Jensen, D. Lapp, & J. Squire (Eds.), Handbook of research on the teaching of the English language arts (pp. 480-501). New York: Macmillan Publishing Company.

Ferguson, S. (1992). Zeroing in on math abilities. Learning, 21, (3), 38-41.

Fogan, W.T. (1989). Empowered students, empowered teachers. The Reading Teacher, 42, 572-78.

Garcia, G.E. (1991). Factors influencing the English reading test performance of Spanish-speaking Hispanic children. Reading Research Quarterly, 25, 371-392.

Garcia, G. & Pearson, P. (1994). Assessment and diversity. In L. Darling-Hammond (Ed.), Review of research in education (pp. 337-391). Washington, DC: American Educational Research Association.

Goodman, Y. (1991). Informal methods of evaluation. In J. Flood, J. Jensen, D. Lapp, and J. Squire (Eds.), Handbook of research on the teaching of the English language arts (pp. 502-509). New York: Macmillan Publishing Company.

Graham, B. (1993). New directions in portfolio assessment: Assessing the assessors. (Report No. 143). Winnipeg, Canada. (ERIC Document Reproduction Service No. ED 355 537).

Hansen, J. (1994). Literacy portfolios: Windows on potential. In S. Valencia, E. Heibert, & P. Afflerbach (Eds.), Authentic reading assessment (pp. 26-45) Newark, DE: International Reading Association.

Hiebert, E. (1991). Teacher-based assessment of literacy learning. In J. Flood, J. Jensen, D. Lapp, & J. Squire (Eds.), Handbook of research on the teaching of the English language arts (pp. 510-520). New York: Macmillan Publishing Company.

Hiebert, E. (1994). Becoming literate through authentic tasks: Evidence and adaptions. In R.B. Ruddell, M.R. Ruddell, & H. Singer (Eds.), Theoretical models and processes of reading (pp. 391-413). Newark, DE: International Reading Association.

Jasmine, J. (1993). Portfolios and other alternative assessments. Westminster, CA: Teacher Created Materials.

Jasmine, J. (1994). Middle school assessment. Westminster, CA: Teacher Created Materials.

References *(cont.)*

Johnston, P. H. (1992). Constructive evaluation of literate activity. New York: Longman.

Johnston, P. H. (1993). Assessment and literate "development." The Reading Teacher, 46, 428-429.

Jongsma, K. (1989). Portfolio assessment. The Reading Teacher, 42, 264-265.

Newkirk, T. (1991). The middle class and the problem of pleasure. In N. Atwell (Ed.), Workshop 3: The politics of process (pp. 63-72). Portsmouth, NH: Heinemann.

Paulson, P.R. & Paulson, F. L. (1991). Portfolios: Stories of knowing. In P. Dreyer (Ed.), Knowing: The power of stories (pp. 294- 303). Claremont, CA: Claremont Reading Conference.

Paulson, F.L., Paulson, P.R., & Meyer, C. (1991). What makes a portfolio a portfolio? Educational Leadership, 48(5), 60-63.

Pearson, P.D. (1994). Integrated language arts. In L. Morrow, J. Smith, & L.C. Wilkinson (Eds.), Integrated language arts: Controversy to consensus (pp.11-32). Boston, MA: Allyn and Bacon.

Ruddell, R. & Unrau, N. (1994). Reading as a meaning construction process: The reader, the text, and the teacher. In R.B. Ruddell, M.R. Ruddell, & H. Singer (Eds.), Theoretical models and processes of reading (pp. 996-1056). Newark, DE: International Reading Association.

Ryan, C. (1994). Social studies assessment: Grades 1-2. Westminster, CA: Teacher Created Materials.

Smith, J. (1994). Standardized testing versus authentic assessment: Godzilla meets Winnie the Pooh. In L. Morrow, J. Smith, & L.C. Wilkinson (Eds.), Integrated language arts: Controversy to consensus (pp. 215-229). Boston, MA: Allyn and Bacon.

Tierney, R. (1994). Learner-based assessment: Making evaluation fit with teaching and learning. In L. Morrow, J. Smith, & L. Wilkinson (Eds.), Integrated language arts: Controversy to consensus (pp. 231-240). Boston, MA: Allyn and Bacon.

Valencia, S. (1990). A portfolio approach to classroom reading assessment: The whys, whats, and hows. The Reading Teacher, 43, 338-340.

Valencia, S. & Calfee, R. (1991). The development and use of literacy portfolios for students, classes, and teachers. Applied Measurement in Education, 4, 333-345.

Valencia, S. & Place, N. (1994). Literacy portfolios for teaching, learning, and accountability: The Bellevue Literacy Assessment Project. In S. Valencia, E. Heibert, & P. Afflerbach (Eds.), Authentic reading assessment (pp. 134-156). Newark, DE: International Reading Association.

Valencia, S & Place, N. (in press). A study of literacy portfolios for teaching, learning, and accountability.

U.S. Congress, Office of Technology Assessment (1992). Testing in American Schools: Asking the right questions. (OTA-SET-519). Washington, D.C.: U.S. Government Printing Office.

White, E. B. (1952). Charlotte's Web. New York: Harper.

Wiggins, G. (1989). Glossary of useful terms related to authentic and performance assessments. Sacramento, CA: California Mathematics Council.

Winograd, P. (1994). Developing alternative assessments: Six problems worth solving. The Reading Teacher, 47, 420-422.

References *(cont.)*

Wolf, D. (1987). Opening up assessment. Educational Leadership, 47(4), 25-29.
Wolf, D. P. (1989). Portfolio assessment: Sampling student work. Educational Leadership, 46, (7), 35-39.
Wolf, D., LeMahieu, P., & Erish, J. (1992). Good measure: Assessment as a tool for educational reform. Educational Leadership, 49(8), 8-13.
Wolf, K.P. (1993). From informal to informed assessment: Recognizing the role of the class room teacher. Journal of Reading, 36, 518-523.
Worthen, B. (1993). Critical issues that will determine the future of alternative assessment. Phi Delta Kappan, 74, 444-454.

Teacher Created Materials Reference List

TCM #504 Portfolios and Other Assessments

TCM #506 Middle School Assessment

TCM #773 Language Arts Assessment, Grades 1-2
TCM #777 Language Arts Assessment, Grades 3-4
TCM #781 Language Arts Assessment, Grades 5-6

TCM #772 Social Studies Assessment, Grades 1-2
TCM #776 Social Studies Assessment, Grades 3-4
TCM #780 Social Studies Assessment, Grades 5-6

TCM #771 Science Assessment, Grades 1-2
TCM #775 Science Assessment, Grades 3-4
TCM #779 Science Assessment, Grades 5-6

TCM #770 Math Assessment, Grades 1-2
TCM #774 Math Assessment, Grades 3-4
TCM #778 Math Assessment, Grades 5-6

TCM Workshop "Portfolios and Other Alternative Assessments"